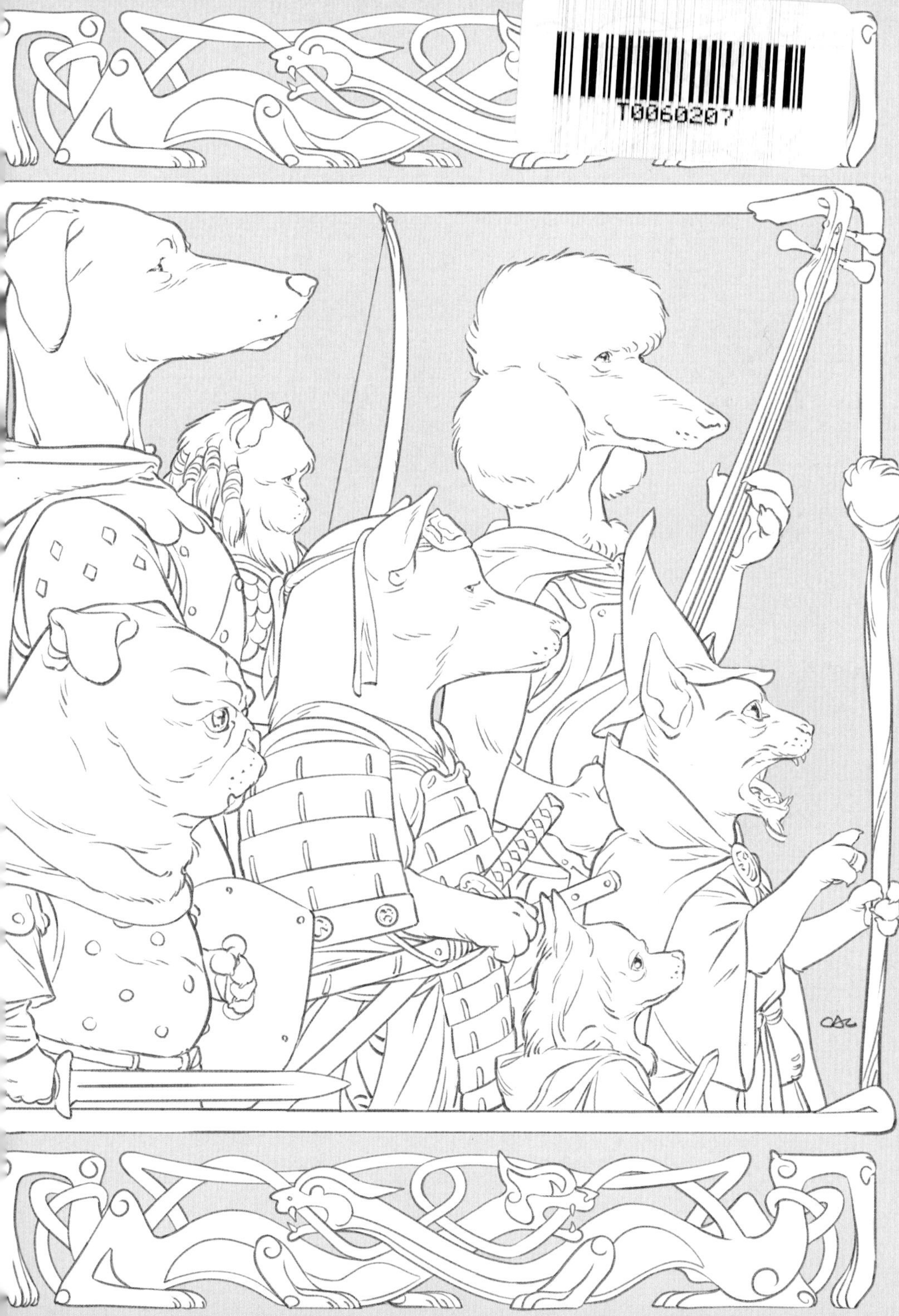

To Morgan.
My best friend
who had a happy 'tail wag'
every time I came home...
A. E.

To Pinky and Perky.
My wonderful girls.
Thank you for all the
bleps, plurps and snuggles.
R. P.

To Po.
The Amazing Dog-Cat.
C. A. W.

To Bono and Tango,
who went on before.
I'll be seeing you.
A. de C.

Written by
Andi Ewington &
Rhianna Pratchett

Illustrated by
Calum Alexander Watt

Edited by
Alex de Campi

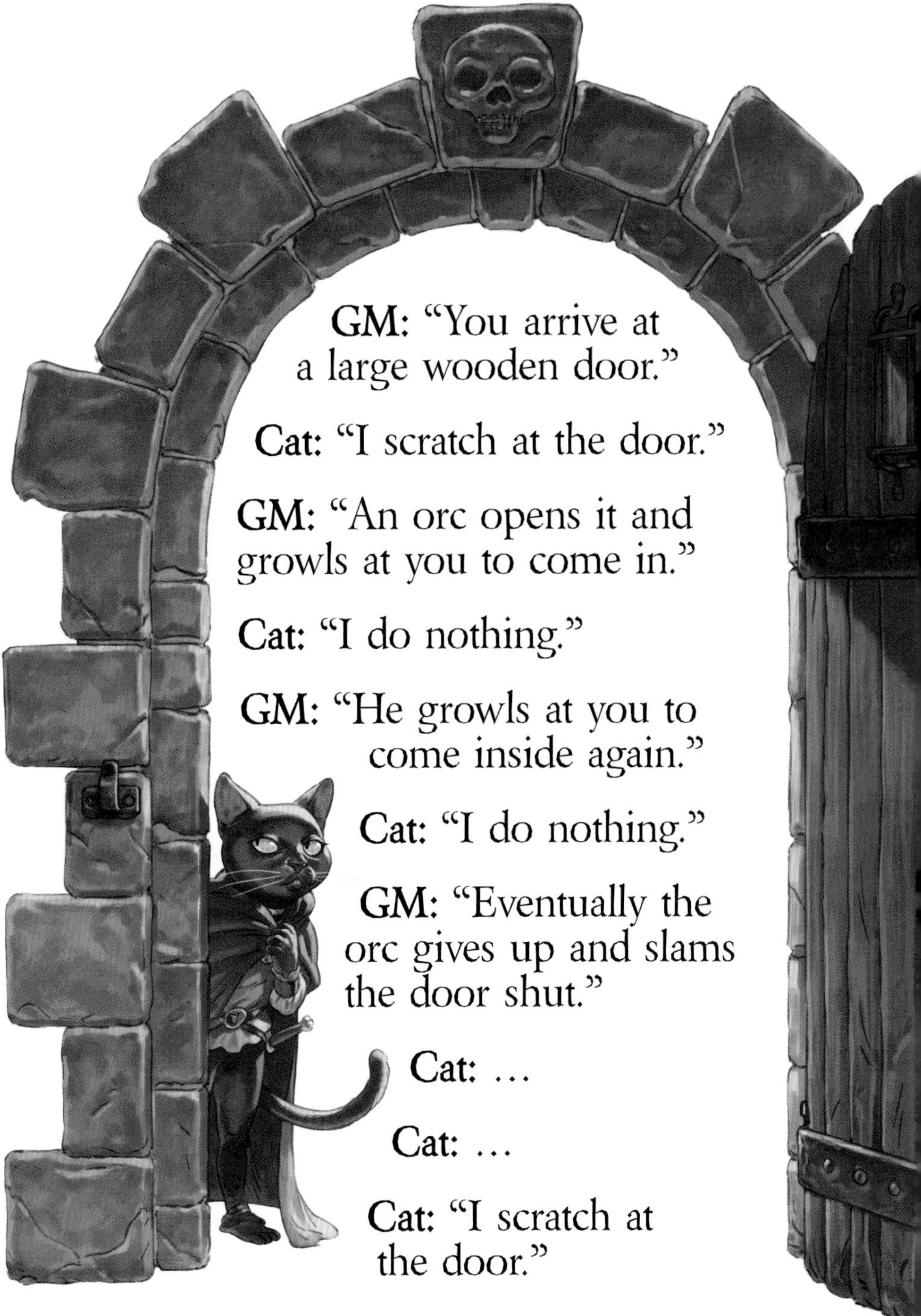

GM: "You arrive at a large wooden door."

Cat: "I scratch at the door."

GM: "An orc opens it and growls at you to come in."

Cat: "I do nothing."

GM: "He growls at you to come inside again."

Cat: "I do nothing."

GM: "Eventually the orc gives up and slams the door shut."

Cat: …

Cat: …

Cat: "I scratch at the door."

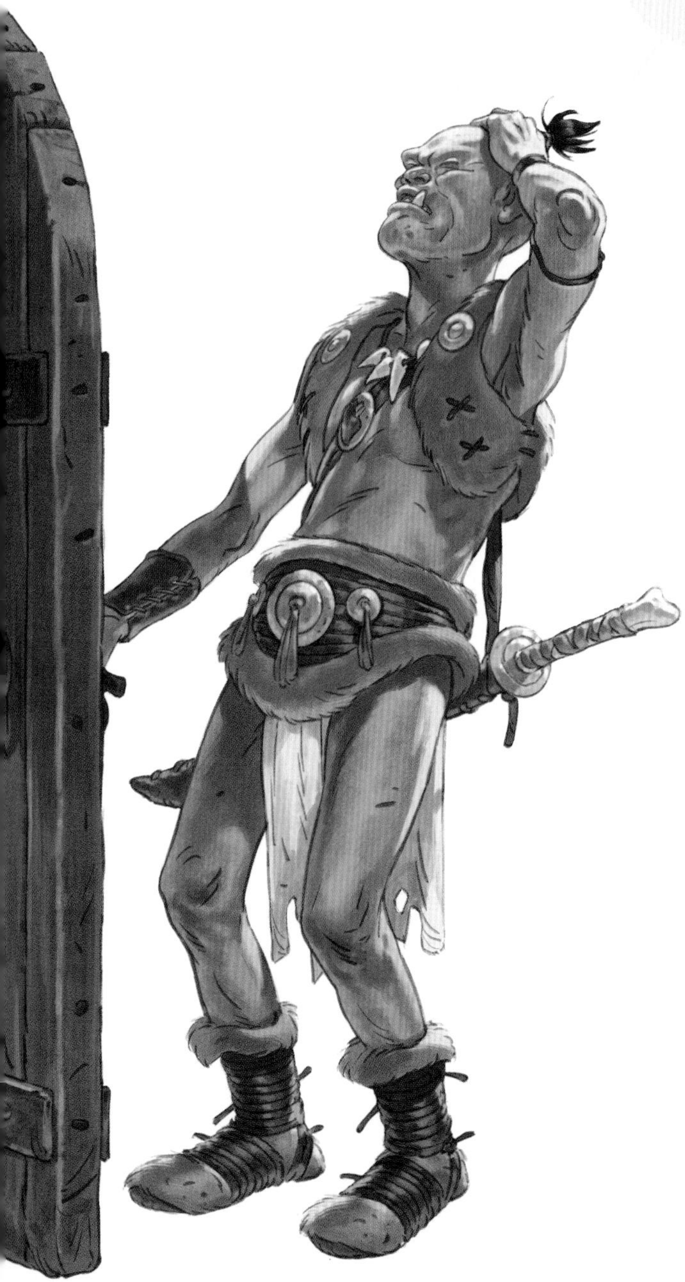

GM: "Trapped inside the gelatinous cube, your feline companion struggles to escape!"

Cat: "Get me out!"

Dog: "I climb up some rocks and jump onto the cube."

GM: "It wobbles beneath you as you stare down at Cat's horrified face."

Dog: "Ooh, it's... *springy.*"

Cat: "Do something! I... I can't feel my paws!"

Dog: "I begin to bounce—"

Cat: "You *WHAT?!*"

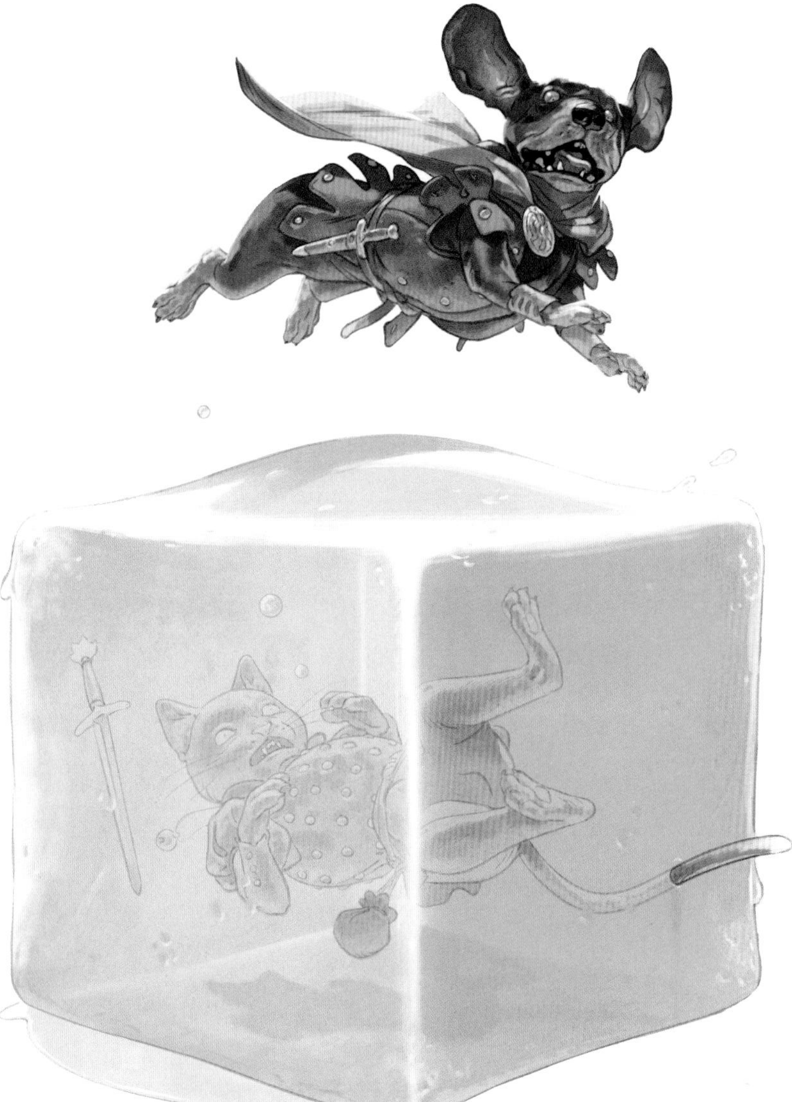

GM: "The orc lies sleeping. There's a metal helmet and a sack of gold beside him."

Parrot: *(whispers)* "Let's take the sack."

GM: "Roll the dice."

Parrot: "Yes, a 12!"

GM: "As you carefully pick up the sack, the gold inside clinks, and the orc stirs. He will wake soon."

Parrot: *(hisses)* "Let's go!"

Cat: "Hang on a moment! Pass me his helmet… and wait outside."

Parrot: *(whispers)* "What are you doing?"

Cat: "Leaving him a little thank-you present."

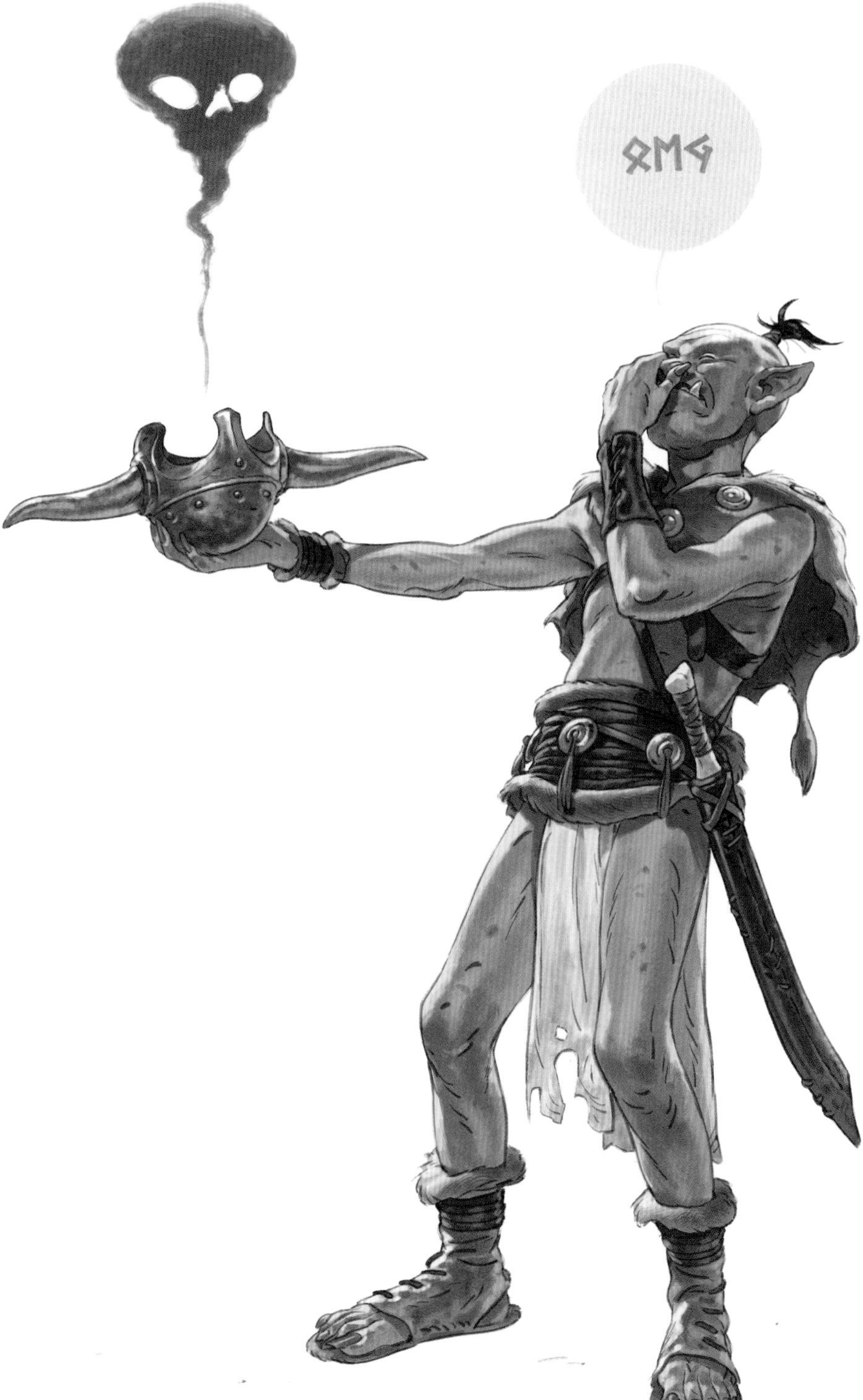

GM: "A new adventurer wants to join your party."

Cat: "Uh, really? Don't take this the wrong way, but…"

Spider: "I *refuse* to be stereotyped."

Dog: "Do you have any useful skills?"

Spider: "I have the best Perception of anyone here, there's nothing I can't climb, and I have an inexhaustible supply of rope…"

Dog: "Oh great! that'd be usef—"

Spider: "…from my bum."

Cat: "OBJECTION!"

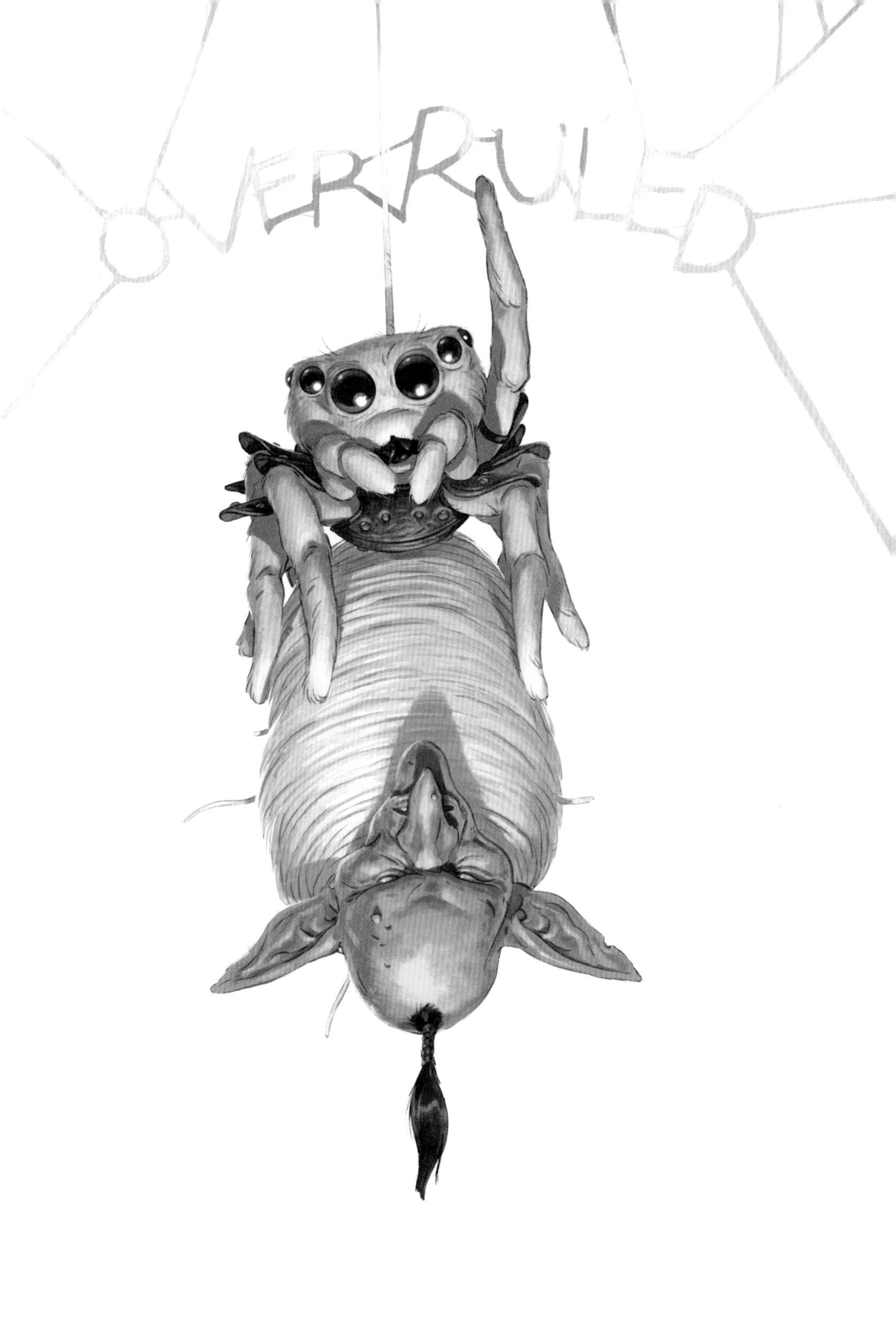
OVERRULED

GM: "You open the chest and find it filled with precious gems and gold coins—"

Cat: "I take everything out of the chest."

GM: "Okaaay, it's now empty—"

Cat: "I get in."

GM: "What?"

Cat: "I climb into the chest."

GM: "Okay… and then what?"

Cat: "I sit."

GM: *(sighs)*

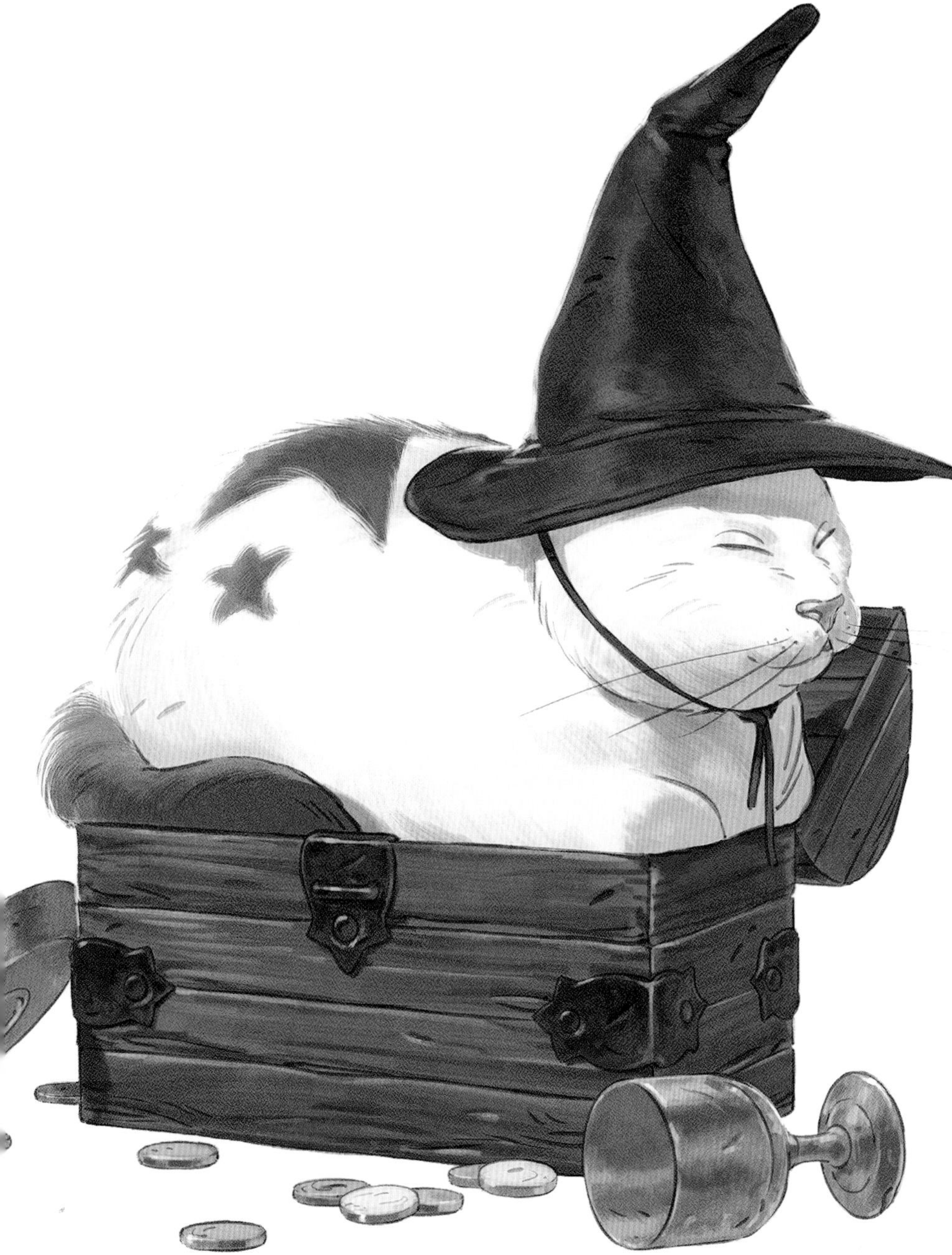

GM: "Cat, your *fireball* does nothing to the hill giant."

Gerbil #1: "Is it my turn yet?"

Cat: "Against a *giant?*"

Gerbil #2: "What about me?"

Cat: "But..."

Gerbil #3: "And me!"

Cat: "Hang on..."

Gerbil #4: "Don't forget me!"

Gerbil #5: "I got 17 for initiative!"

Cat: "...weren't there only *two* of you when we started this campaign?"

Gerbil #1: *(shrugs)* "We've been busy."

Gerbil #2: "Right, family. Get him!"

Gerbil #3: "Go for the eyes!"

Gerbil #4: "No! Go for *everything!*"

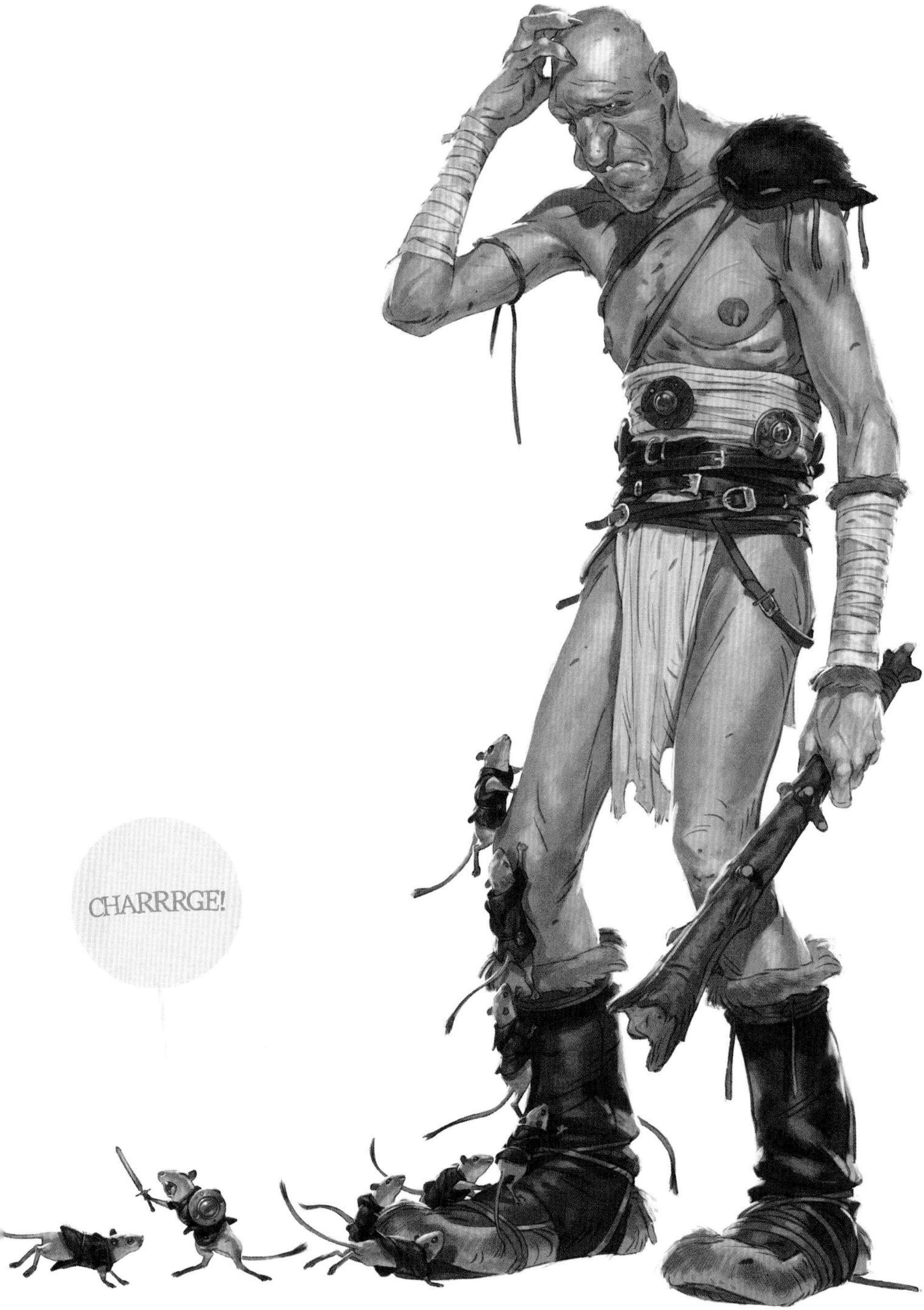
CHARRRGE!

GM: "You come to a narrow passageway."

Dog: "I walk through with my staff held out across my body."

GM: …

GM: "Make a Perception roll."

Dog: "Hmmm… I got a 3."

GM: "You find you can't get through for some reason."

Dog: "Can I try again?"

GM: "Sure."

Dog: "Ouch, a 1…"

Dog: "…Third time lucky?"

GM: *(sighs)* "What's your Intelligence stat?"

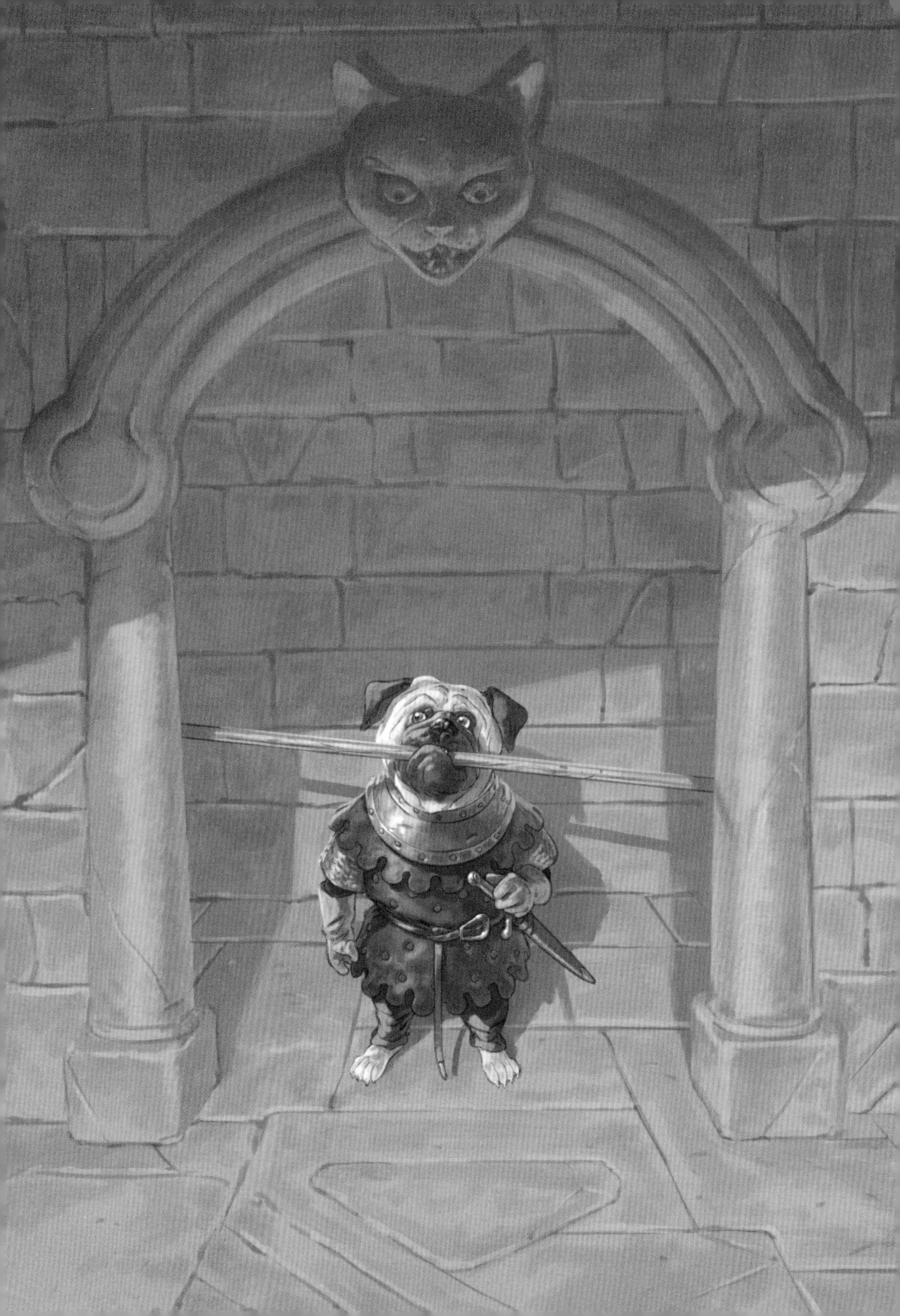

GM: "The ogre lumbers towards your party."

Dog: "I reach for my *hammer of clobbering.* Wait… where is it?"

Cat: "My *dual daggers!* They've gone missing too!"

GM: "Perhaps a thief lurks in the shadows."

Dog: *(sighs)* "Clive, give them *back.*"

Hamster: "I'th ju'th keepi'th the' th'afe!"

GM: "With a final roar, the red dragon goes down, slain by a mix of good fortune and steely determination. What do you want to do now?"

Cat: "I grab it by the tail and carry it back to camp."

GM: "What?"

Cat: "I grab it—"

GM: "It weighs over 15 tonnes!"

Cat: "I. Grab. It."

GM: "Fine, you know what? Roll against Strength."

Cat: *(grins)* "Natural 20!"

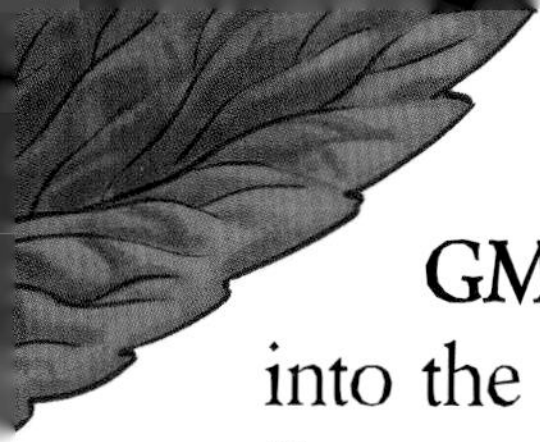

GM: "You follow the kobold party's tracks into the eerily silent Milkwood Forest, where they disappear into its lush undergrowth."

Cat: "I search for herbs."

GM: "Erm… sure, which herb are you searching for?"

Cat: "Catnip."

GM: "Okay, roll Survival to forage."

Cat: "I got 17!"

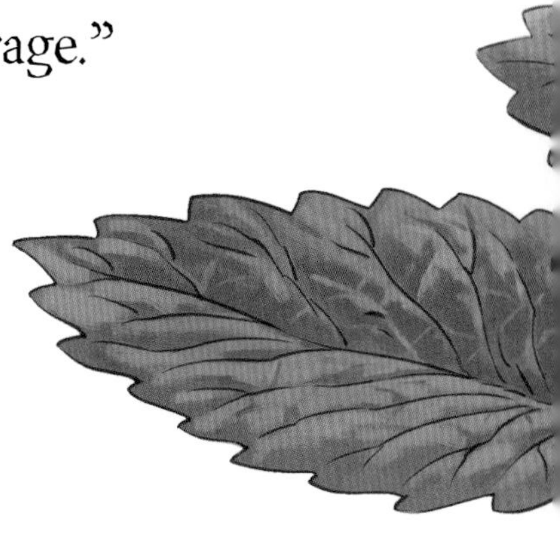

GM: "Success! You find exactly what you're looking for—"

Cat: "I cast *plant growth* on the catnip."

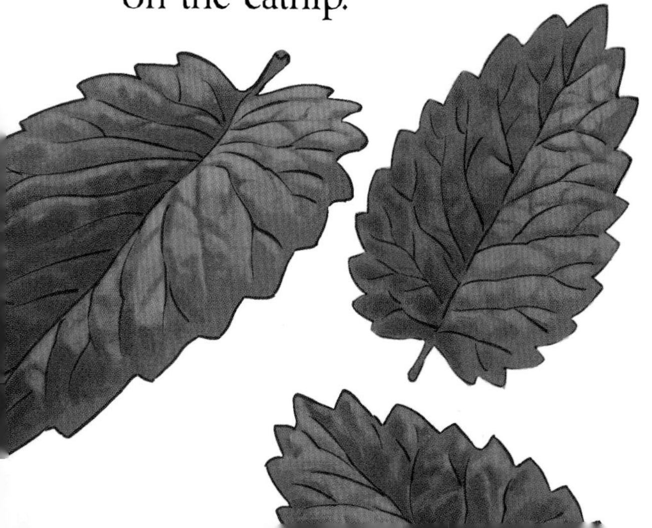

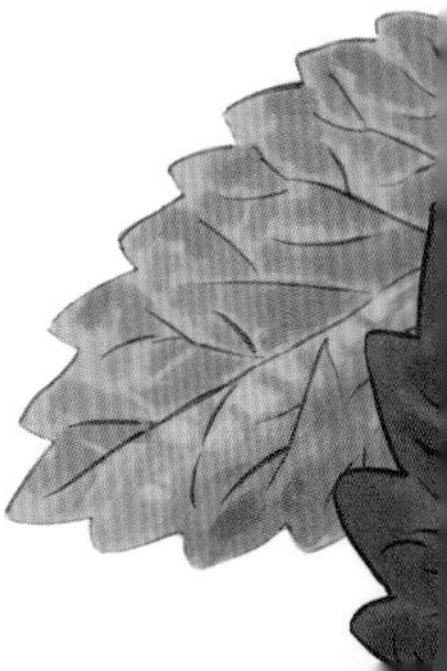

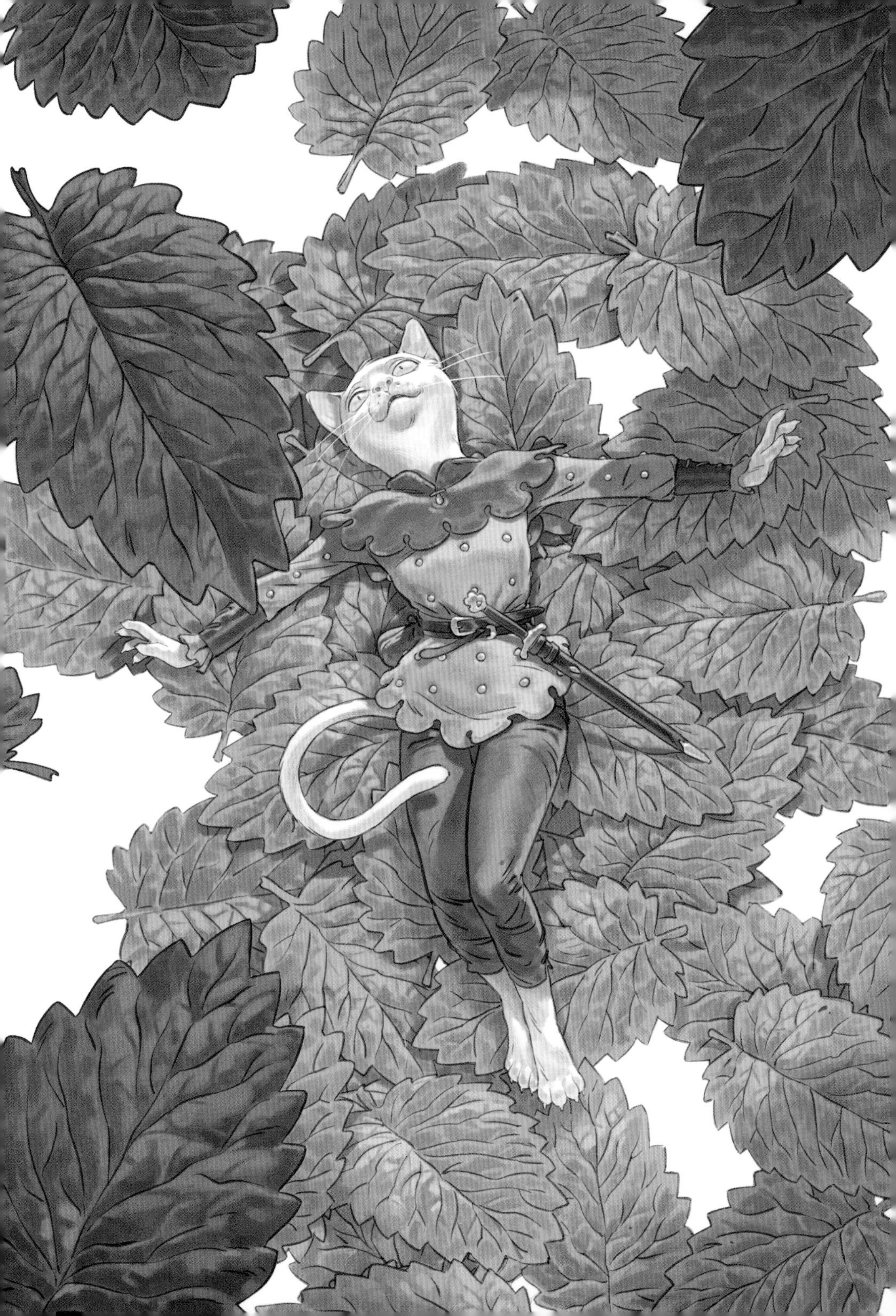

GM: "You see a goblin war party sitting around a campfire eating supper."

Dog: "I go into camp and stare at whatever they're eating."

GM: *(rolls for goblin reaction)* "By some miracle they just stare back at you."

Dog: "I beg for their food."

GM: *(sighs)* "Make a Charisma roll with disadvantage."

Dog: "A 20 and… another 20!"

GM: "Sonofa—"

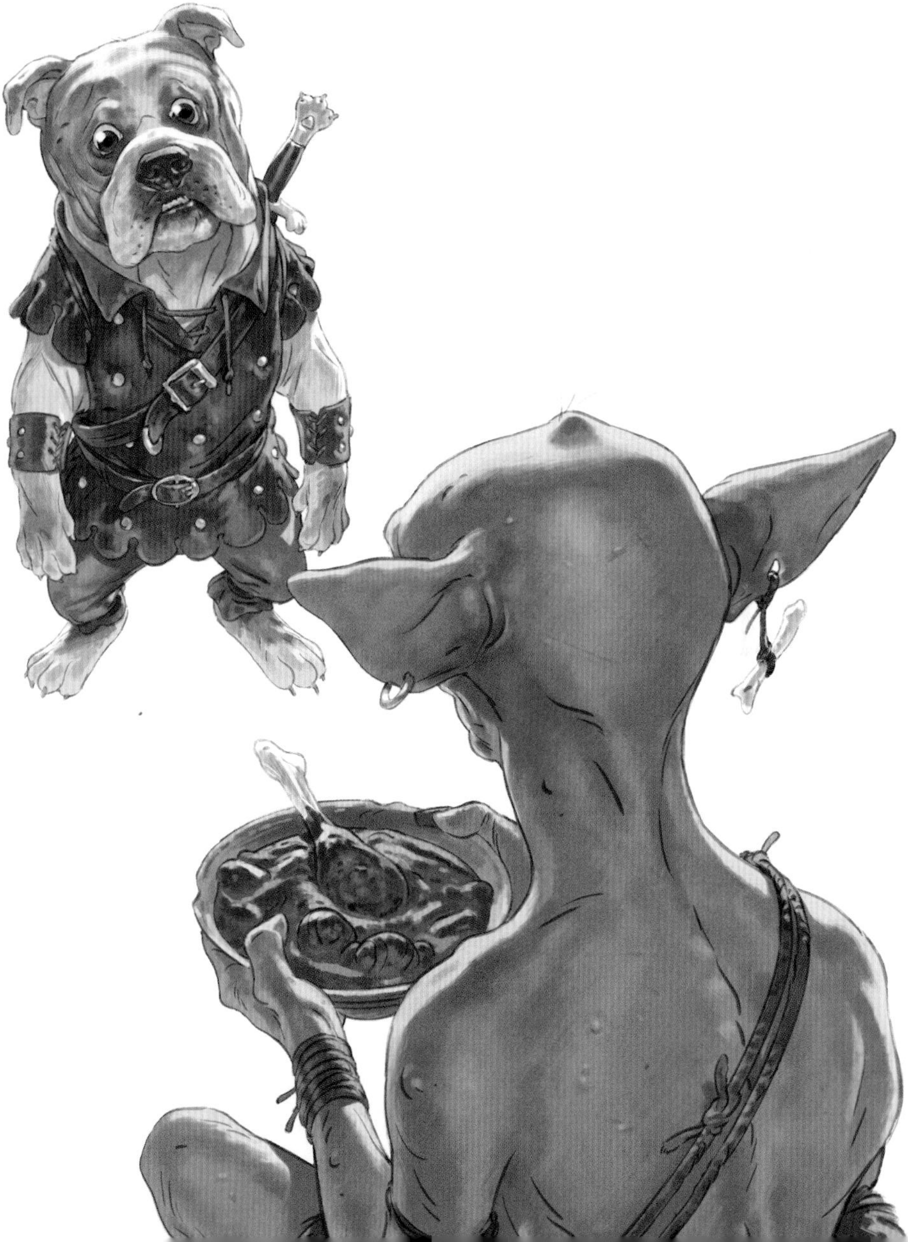

GM: "You come upon the dragon's lair."

Rat: "Let's loot it!"

Chameleon: "All right!"

GM: "There's a roar."

Rat: "I roll Stealth to hide."

Chameleon: "I use my camouflage ability."

GM: "The dragon lumbers in and sniffs the air."

Dragon: "…Quentin?"

Chameleon: "*Derek?* Is that you?"

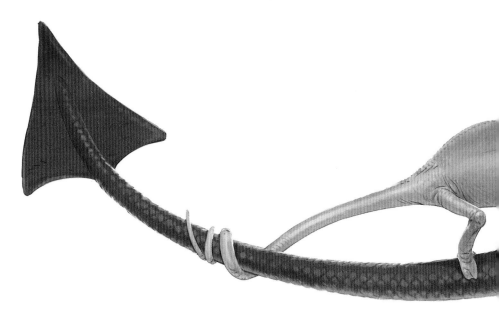

Dragon: "Mate! I've not seen you since Draconic University."

Chameleon: "Dropped out, didn't I. Never could get the roaring right."

Dragon: "Fancy a pint?"

Chameleon: "Epic! Let's hit the tavern!"

Rat: "Hey! Wait for me!"

GM: "The fairy princess thanks you and your party of heroes for rescuing her people from the evil ice trolls. Her kin have been spared from slavery, torture and a cold grave. Your selfless bravery will echo for eternity in their songs. The fairy princess will now grant you three wishes—"

Cat: "I eat the fairy."

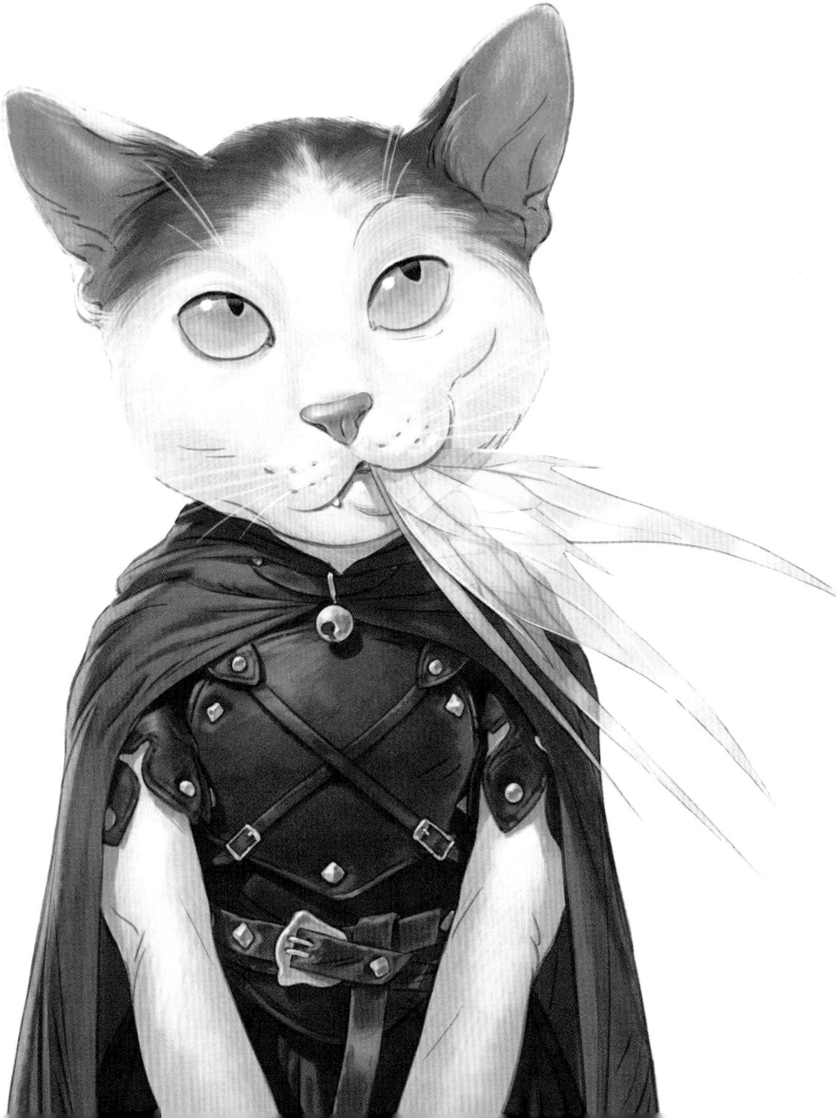

GM: "Who will take on the demon?"

Rabbit: "I step forward."

GM: "The demon looks down at you and laughs."

Dog: "I whisper 'food pellets' in my comrade's ear."

Rabbit: *(nose twitches in agitation)* "Eurgh."

Dog: "Empty water bottles!"

Rabbit: *(foams at the mouth)* "Nnngh!"

GM: "The demon stops laughing and looks perplexed."

Dog: "Tiny, cramped hutches!"

Rabbit: *(gripped by fury)* "BERSERKER RAGE!"

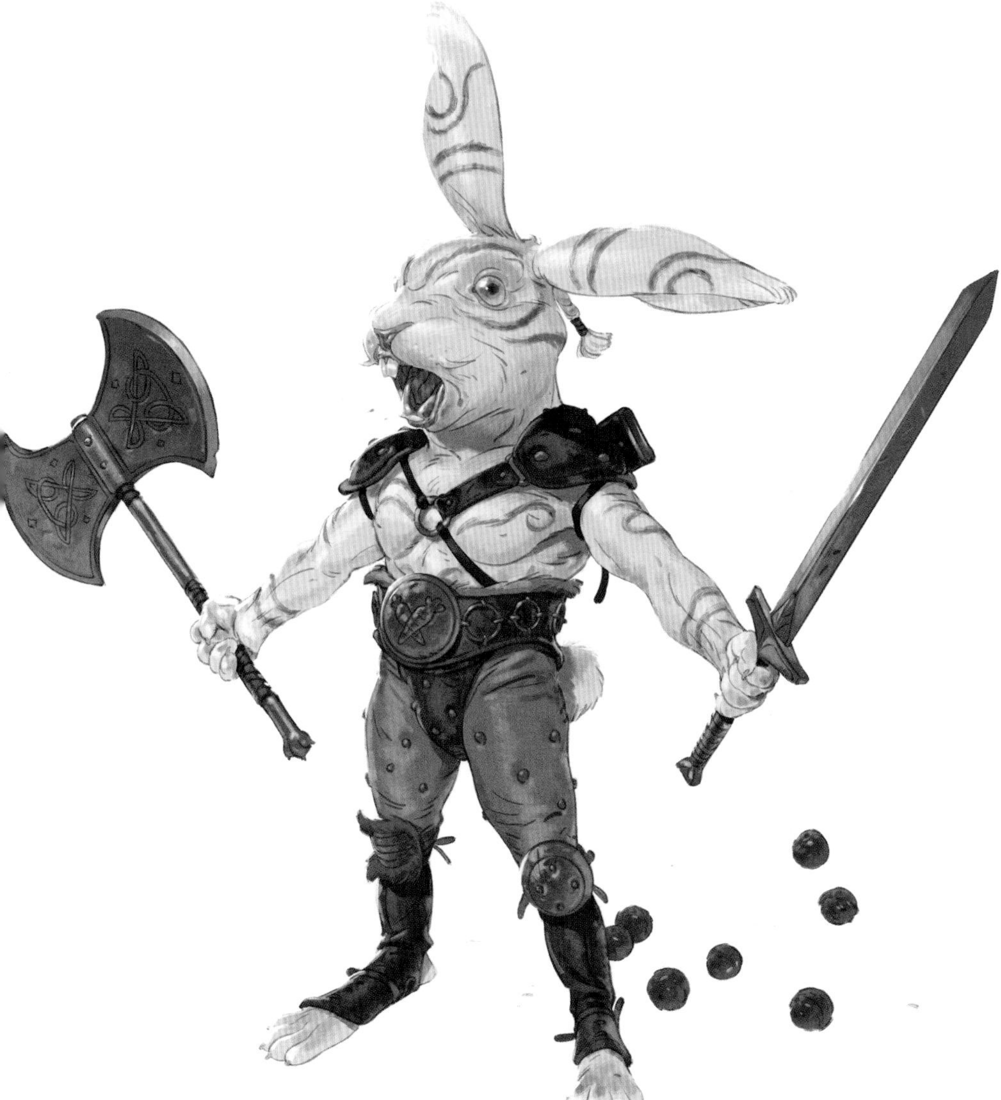

GM: "You come to a dead end. There's nothing here but a small hole—"

Cat: "I go in the hole."

GM: "Make a Wisdom roll."

Cat: "I don't need to. I go in the hole."

GM: "But you're wearing plate—"

Cat: "I go in the hole."

GM: "You're never going to fit—"

Cat: "I. Go. In. The. Hole."

GM: …

GM: *(weary)* "You're stuck."

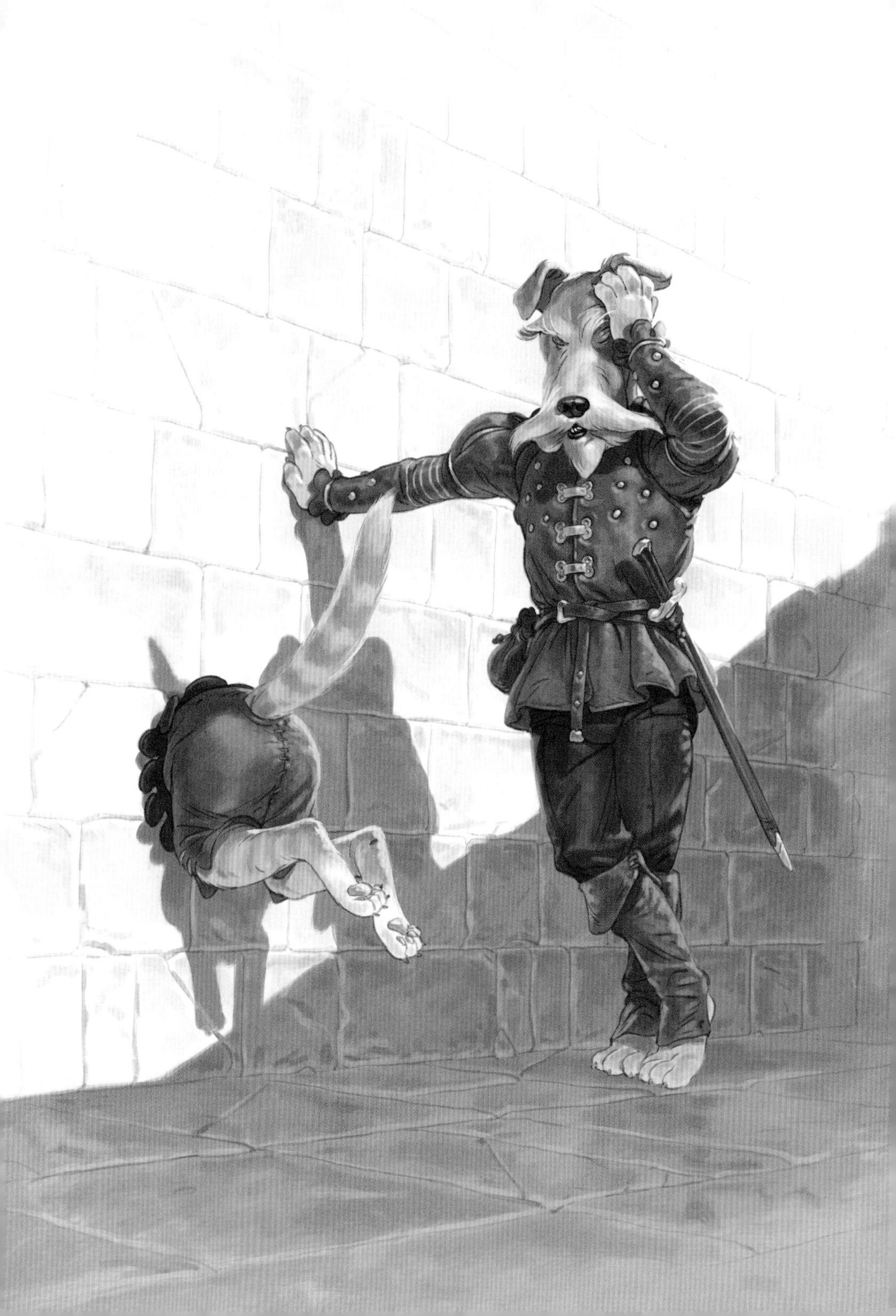

GM: "The first hydra head snaps at you."

Snake: "I sssling a *fireball* towards it."

GM: "Roll for your attack."

Snake: "A 16! Sssmashing!"

GM: "Your *fireball* engulfs the first head in flames. But the second head grabs you. You feel the power of the creature's maw crushing your body."

Snake: "I use my ssshed armour ability."

GM: "You leave it with a mouthful of scales. There's just time enough to grab one thing from the pile of treasure."

Snake: "Sssuper! What did I sssnatch?"

GM: "*Boots of speed.*"

Snake: "…boots?"

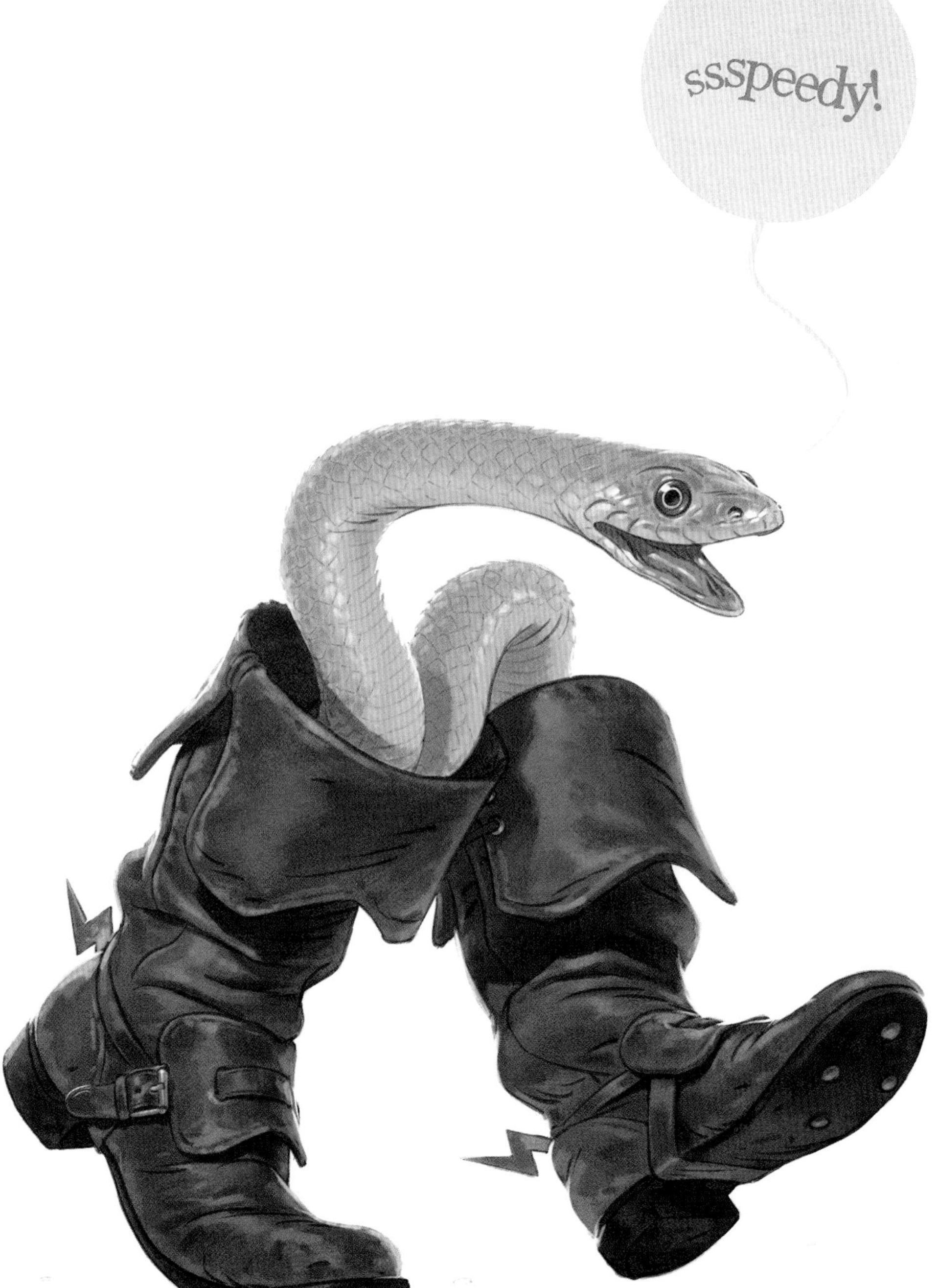
ssspeedy!

GM: "From your hiding spot, you see an orc bent over his fallen comrade. He hasn't noticed you yet."

Dog: "I sneak up from behind."

GM: "Okay, roll Stealth."

Dog: "Yes! An 18!"

GM: "You move quickly and quietly towards the orc. How do you choose to press your advantage?"

Dog: "I sniff his bum."

GM: …

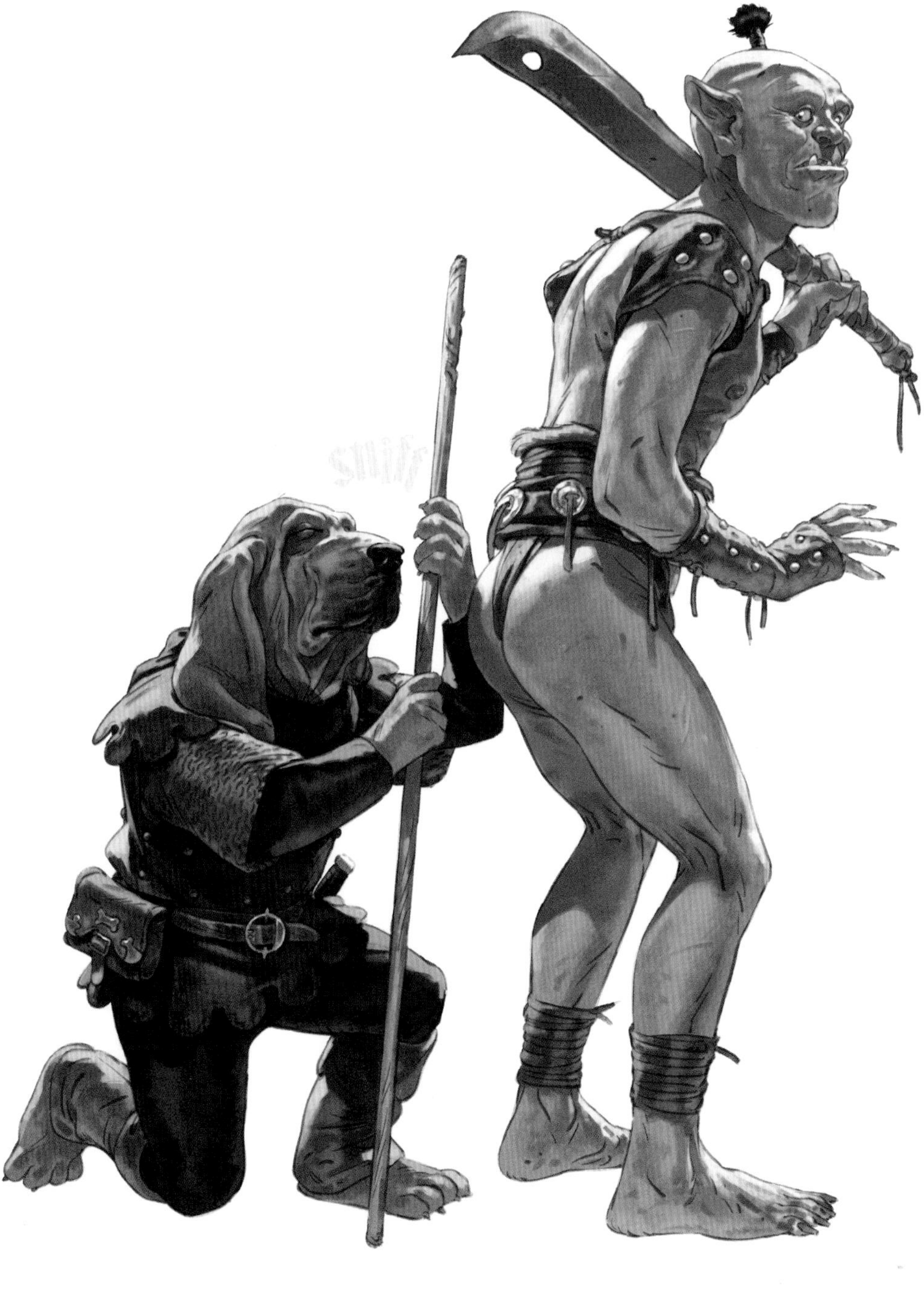
sniff

GM: "As the goblin army strides forward, your spirits are as broken as your swords and bows."

Dog: "We do have *one* weapon left…"

GM: "...You do?"

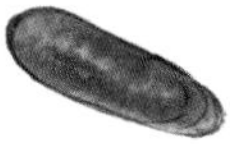

Guinea Pig: "I have never been more ready!"

Dog: "I pick up Guinea Pig and get into firing position."

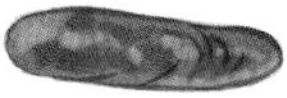

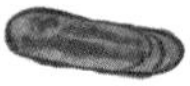

Guinea Pig: "Locked and loaded! I lift my battle kilt."

Dog: "Say hello to my little friend!"

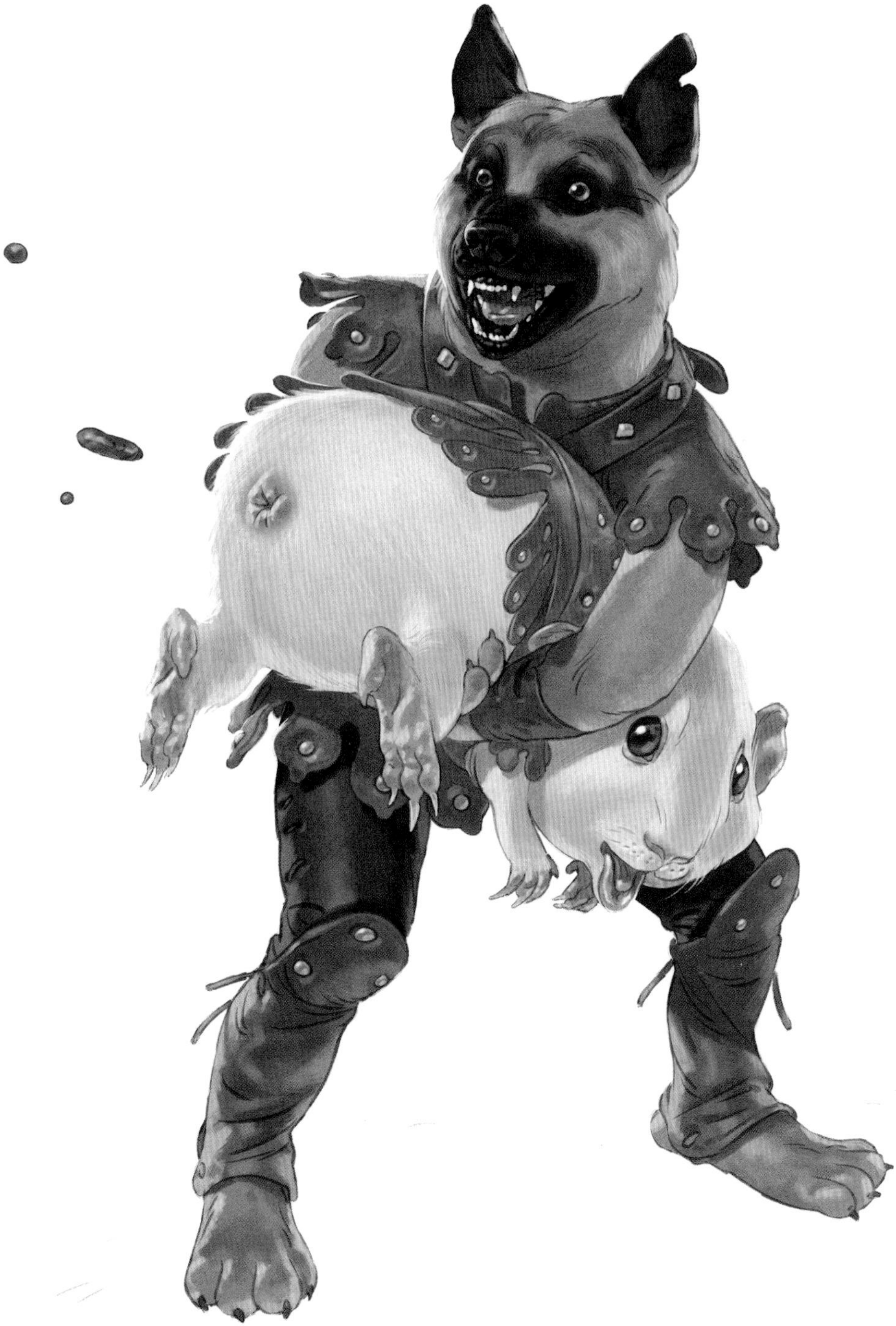

GM: "You enter the Snuggly Duckling tavern for a well-earned drink and perhaps some information on where the dark mage has fled. But the landlord, a gruff dwarf, seems less than pleased to see you."

Cat: "I'll be cordial towards him."

GM: "Make a Charisma roll."

Cat: "I got 15."

GM: "Success! The dwarf smiles as he warms to you."

Cat: "I scratch his eyes out."

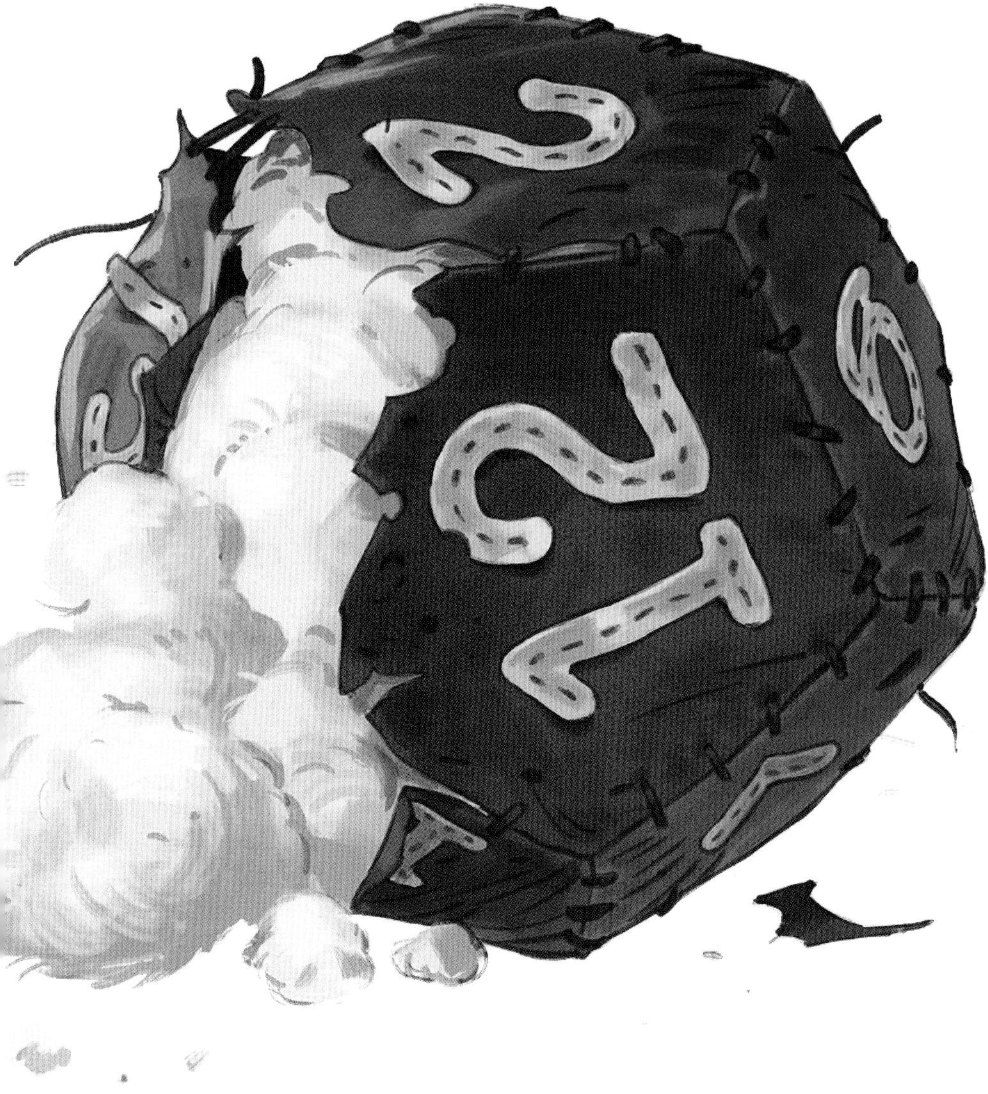

GM: "The castle gates stand firm. No weapon will breach them. The guards laugh down at you."

Cat: "Right, Tortoise, you're up! Dog, get ready with the *potion of haste.*"

Dog: "Huh? Er, okay."

GM: "What's he going to...?"

Tortoise: "I tighten my helmet around my head."

Cat: "I angle Tortoise towards the gate."

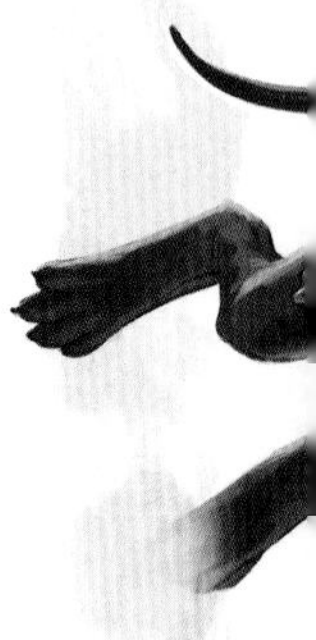

Dog: "I smash the potion against his shell."

Tortoise: "Get on, lads!"

Dog: "Should smoke be coming out of... *there?*"

Tortoise: "Just hold on!"

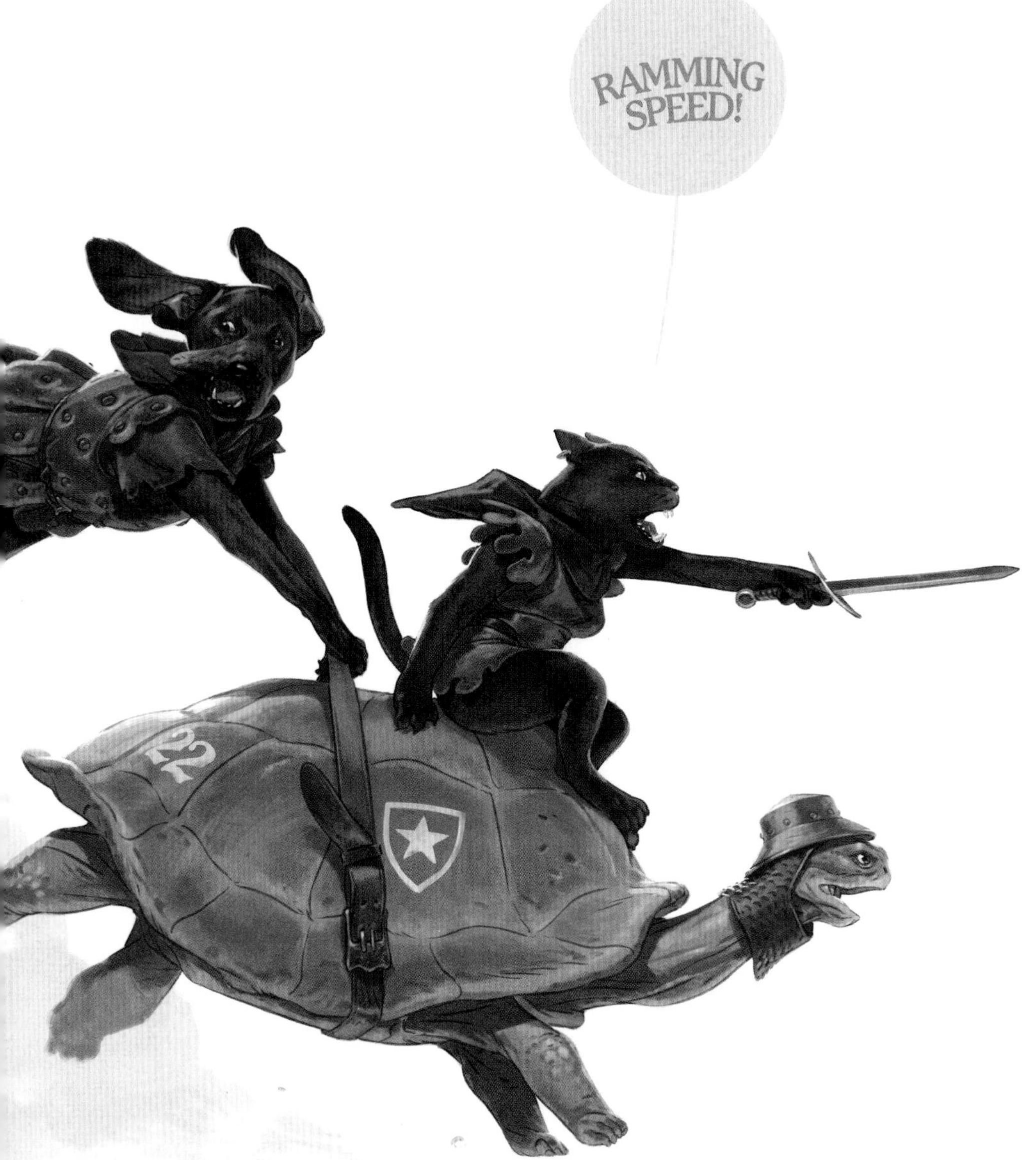
RAMMING SPEED!

GM: "The sorceress carefully places the glowing bottle on the workbench next to her. 'Take heed, brave adventurers,' she intones, 'for contained within this delicate vial is enough power to destroy Hafgan's entire necropolis. If a single drop fell upon the ground it would surely—'"

Cat: "I knock the bottle off the table."

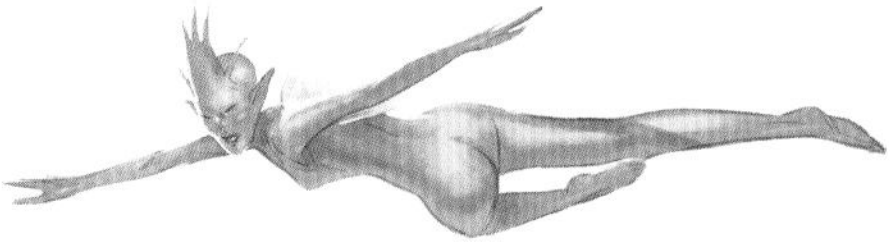

GM: "You have finally slain the beast! The pixie queen is free! She goes to bestow a kiss of thanks on Frog—"

Toad: "Hang on! I won the fight—"

Frog: "Yep! Thanks to your Constitution of 18…"

Toad: "—so how come you get the kiss?"

Frog: "…and your Charisma of 3."

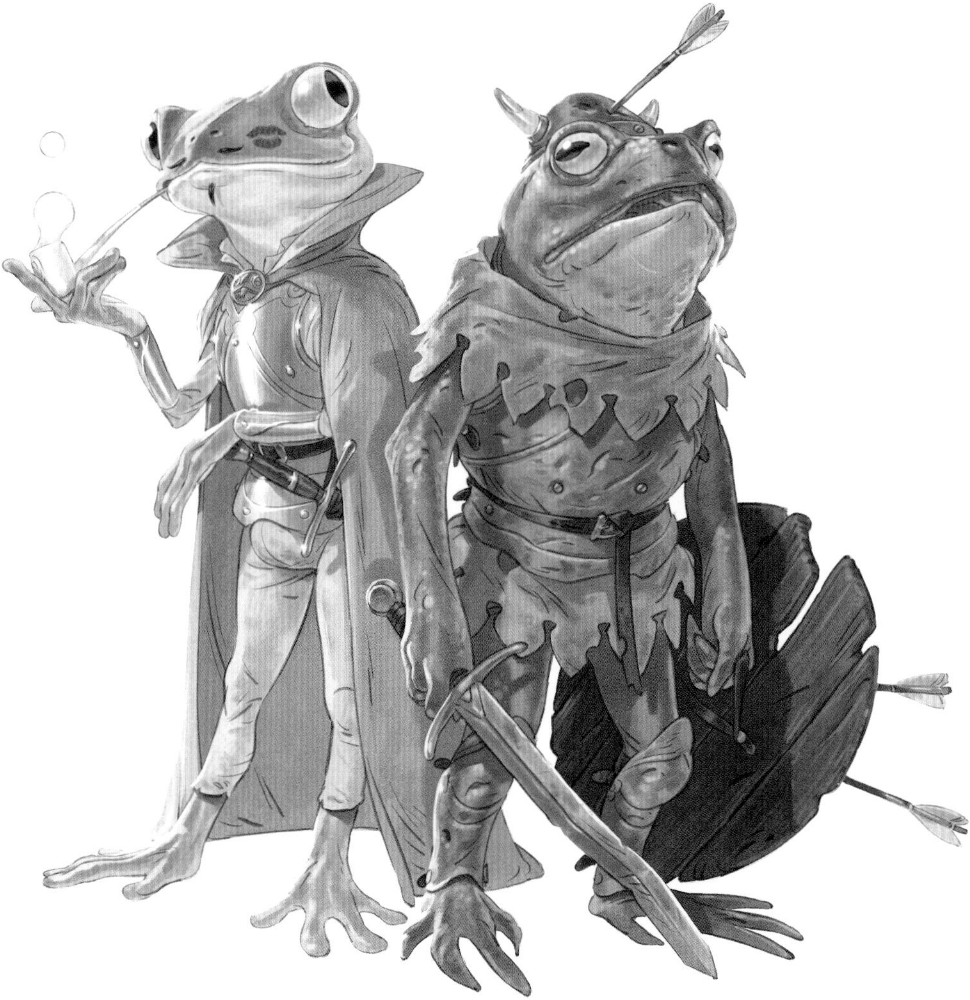

GM: "The orc horde descends on your camp—"

Cat: "We're trapped! We'll have to fight our way out!"

Dog: "I cast an *animal companion* spell."

Cat: "Summon a lion, or a bear! Anything that's big and has sharp teeth and claws!"

Dog: "Nnnh…"

Cat: "Don't you dare—"

GM: …

Dog: *(shaking with nervous energy)* "Sss…"

Cat: "Don't you fu—"

Dog: "…SQUIRREL!"

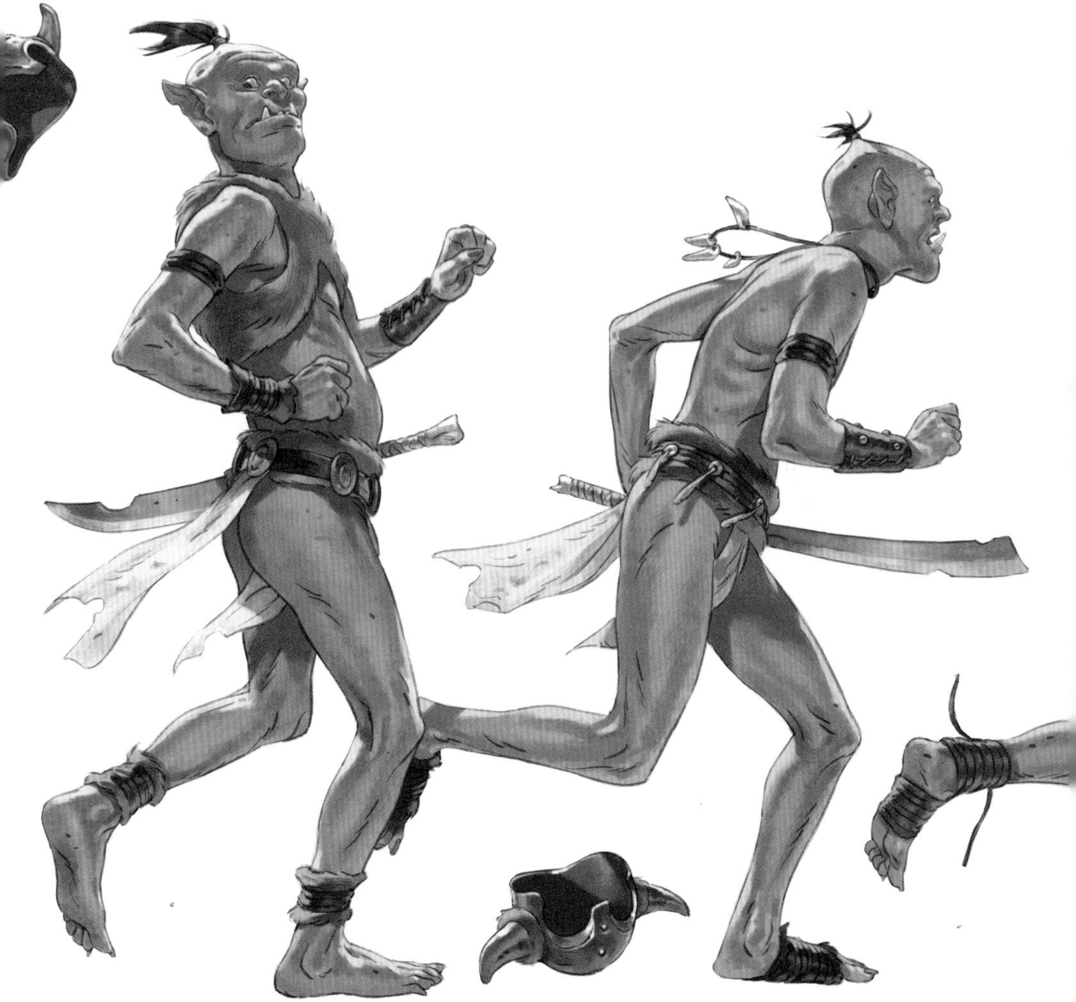

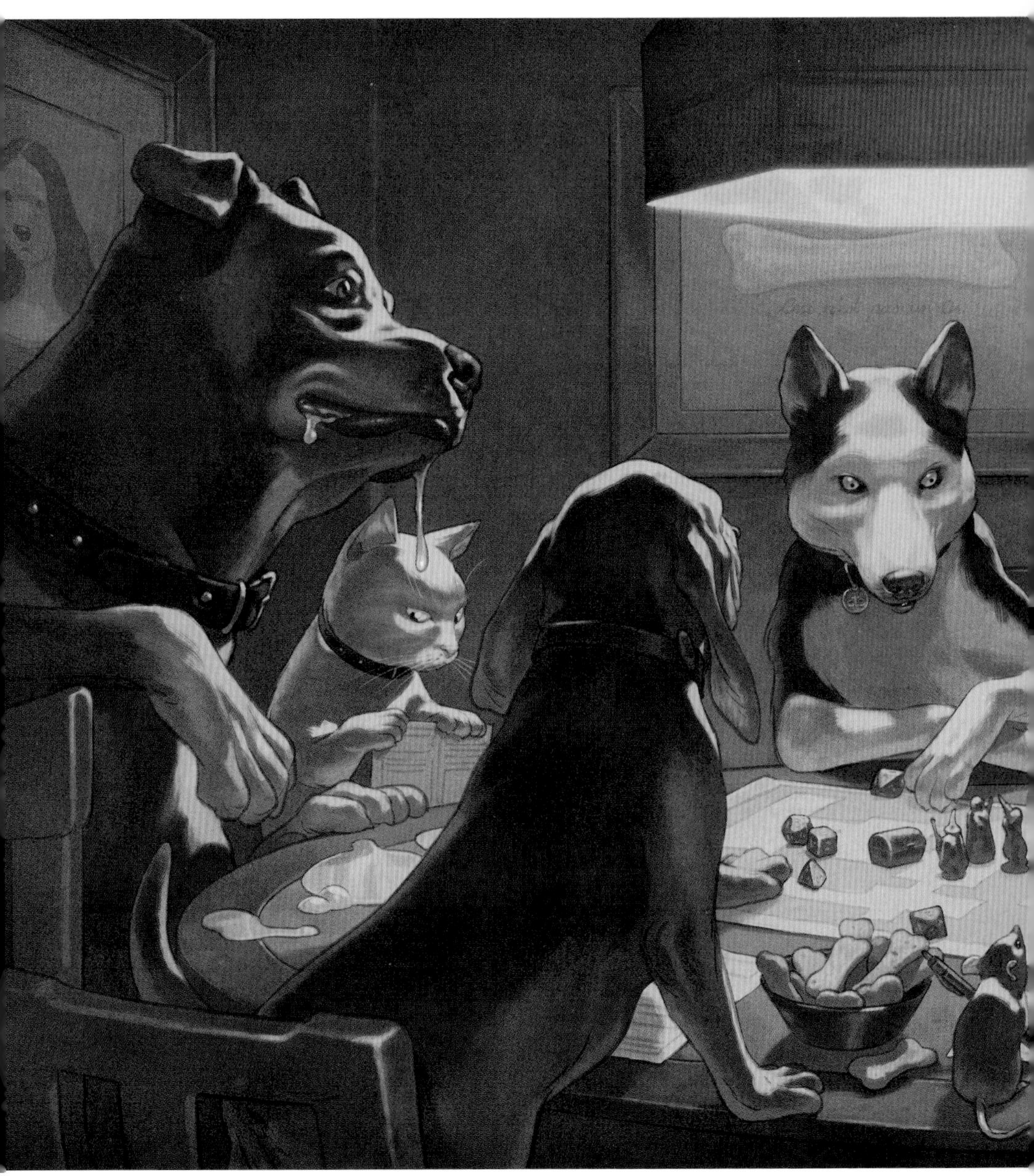

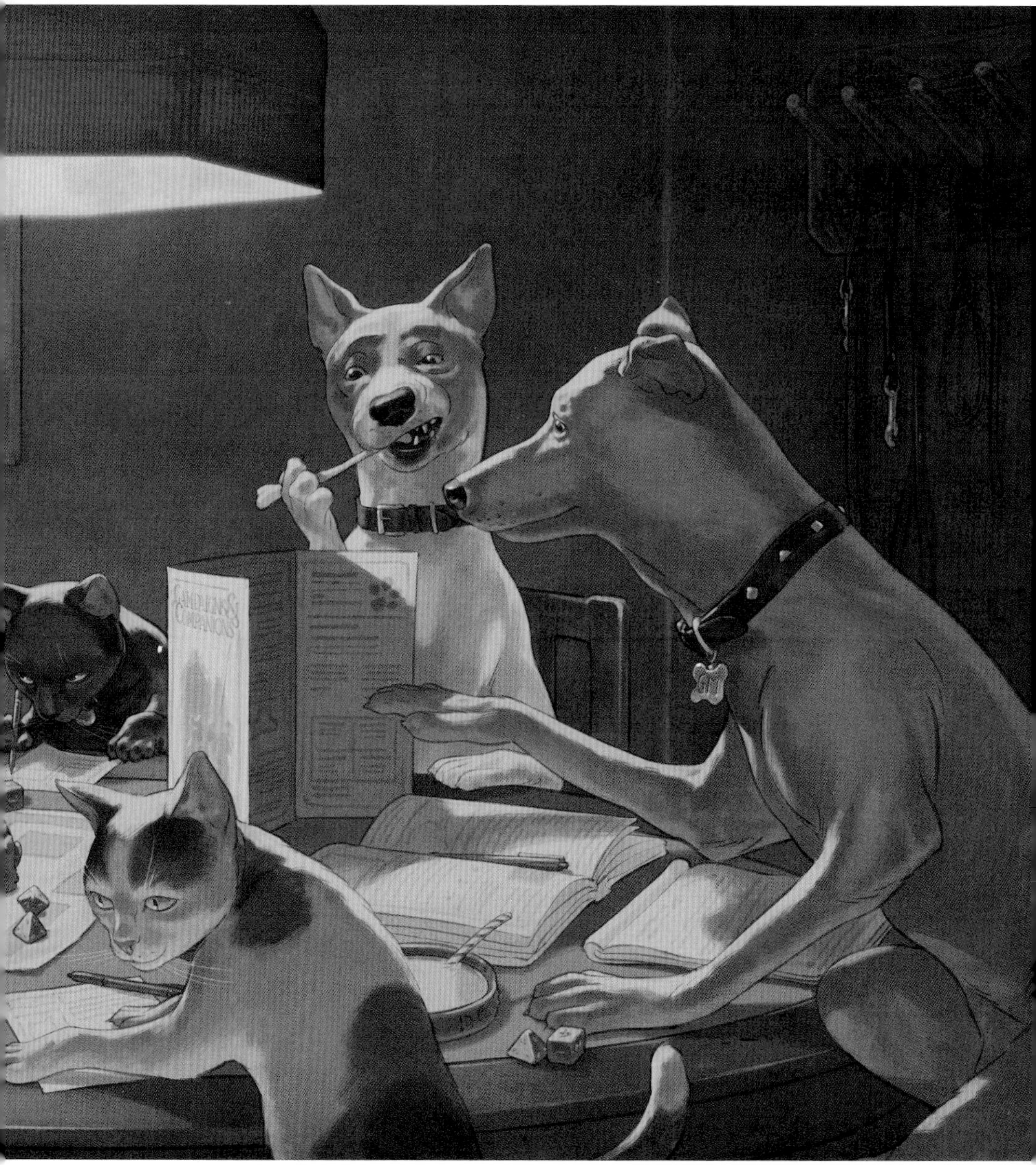

GM: "You arrive at a fast-moving river—"

Cat: "Sorry, what?"

GM: "A fast-moving river."

Cat: "No thank you. Not crossing that."

GM: "Make a Perception roll."

Cat: "I rolled 16."

GM: "You're wise to be hesitant. The river is too dangerous to swim—"

Dog: "I JUMP IN! WHEEEEE!"

Cat: ...

Cat: "Solo campaign?"

GM: *(sighs)* "Sure."

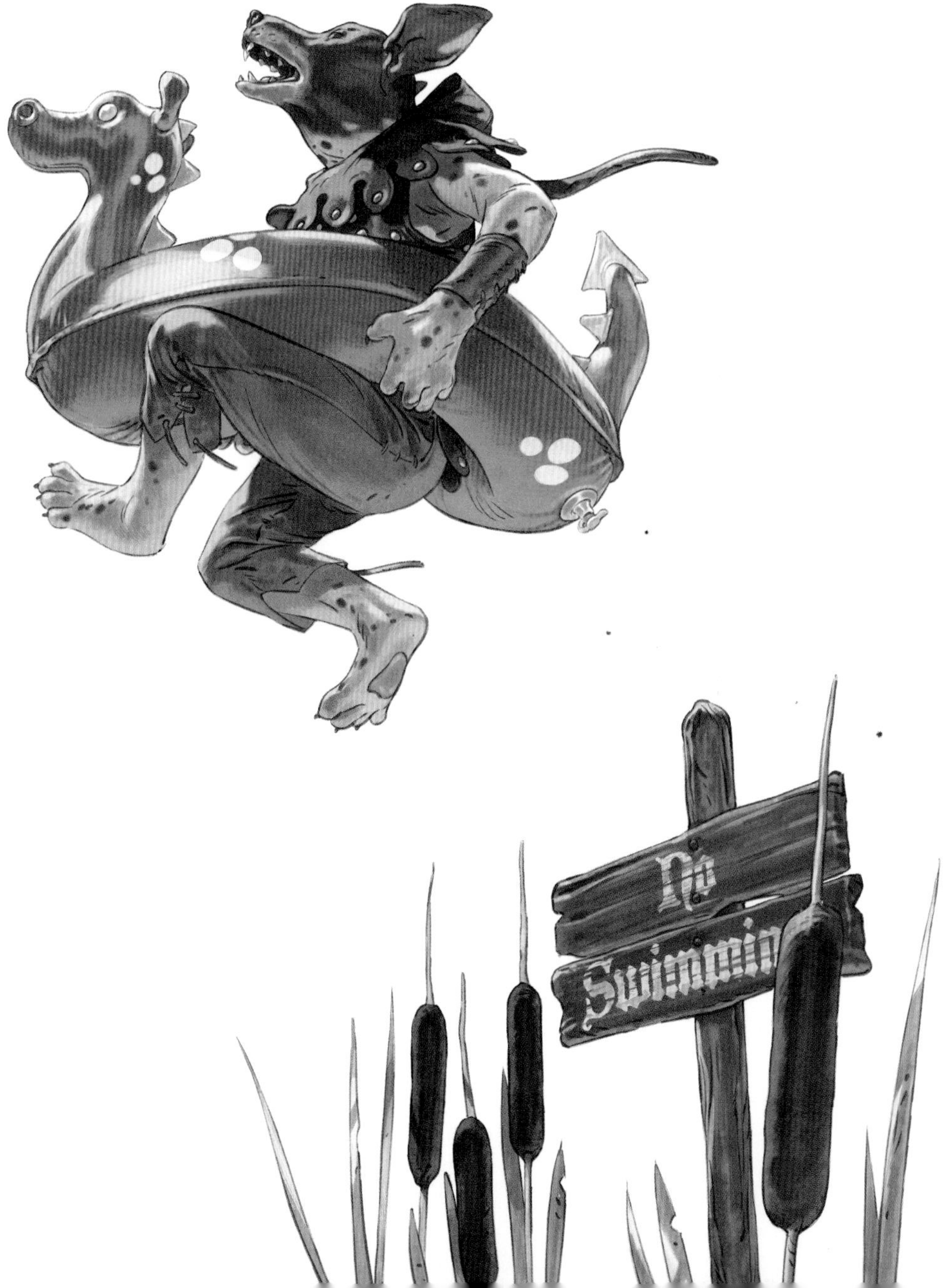
No
Swimmin

Dog: "I want to cast *animal friendship*."

GM: "On what animal?"

Dog: "On Cat!"

Cat: "Hey, I'm a character!"

GM: "I mean, you *are* an animal. Roll Wisdom to save."

Cat: "18, that's a pass."

Dog: "Ulp."

Cat: "I roll up my sleeves..."

Dog: "Uh, Cat..."

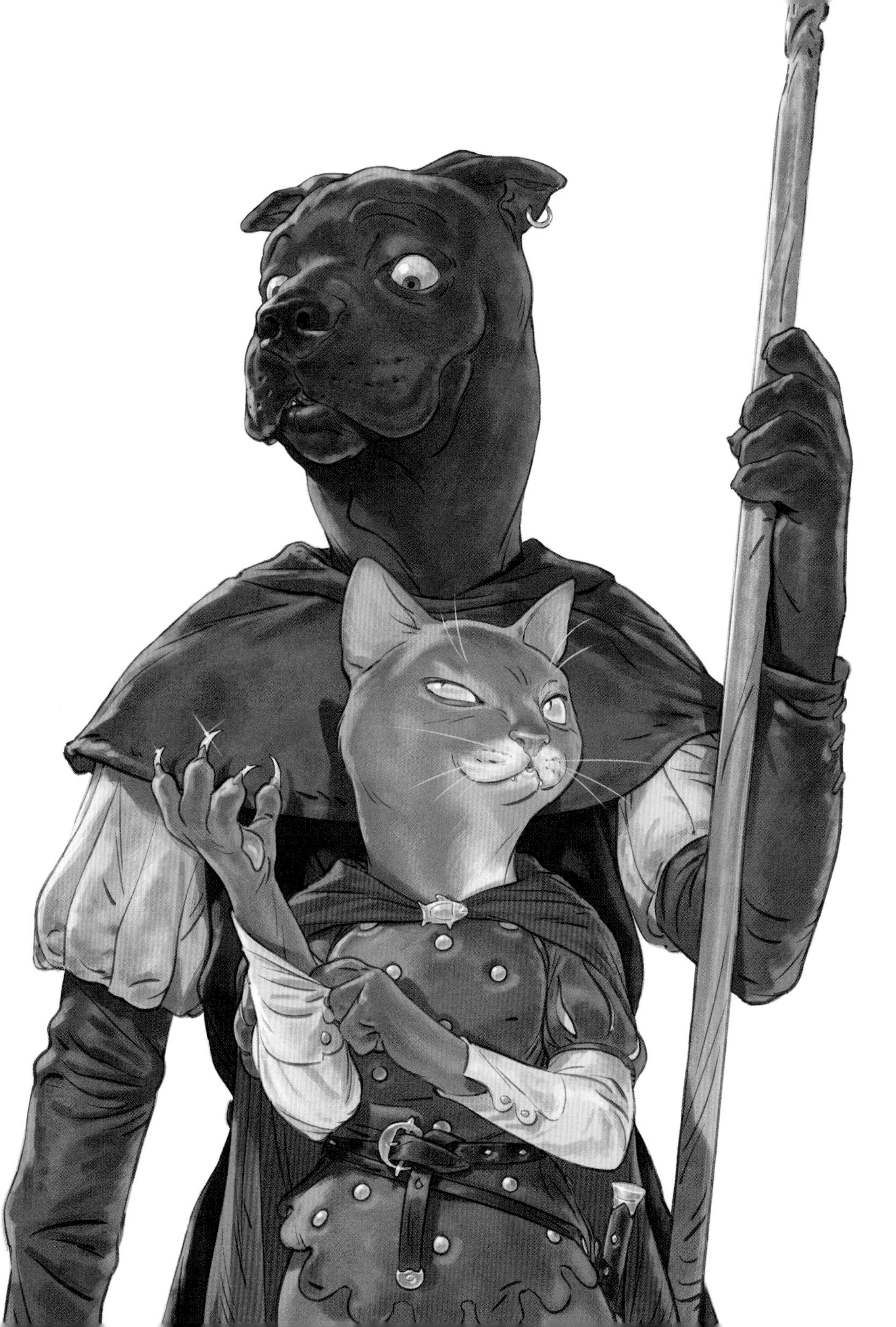

GM: "The dark wizard screams in his death throes, but before he expires, he still manages to cast a *mirror image* spell—"

Cat: "Get ready! There'll be two of him soon!"

GM: "—on Budgie."

Cat: "What?"

Budgie: "On *me?*"

GM: "A 15. Yup."

Budgie: *(to his clone)* "Who's a pretty boy, then?"

Cat: "Stop!"

Budgie: "Who's a pretty boy?"

Cat: *(sighs)*

Cat: "I cast *animate dead* on the mouse."

GM: "The mouse rises, albeit now undead."

Cat: "I kill the mouse."

GM: "What? That's dark. Okay, the mouse 'dies' a second time."

Cat: "I cast *animate dead* on the mouse again."

GM: "What are you doing?"

Cat: "I kill the mouse."

GM: "Stop it!"

Cat: "I cast *animate dead* on the mouse…"

GM: …

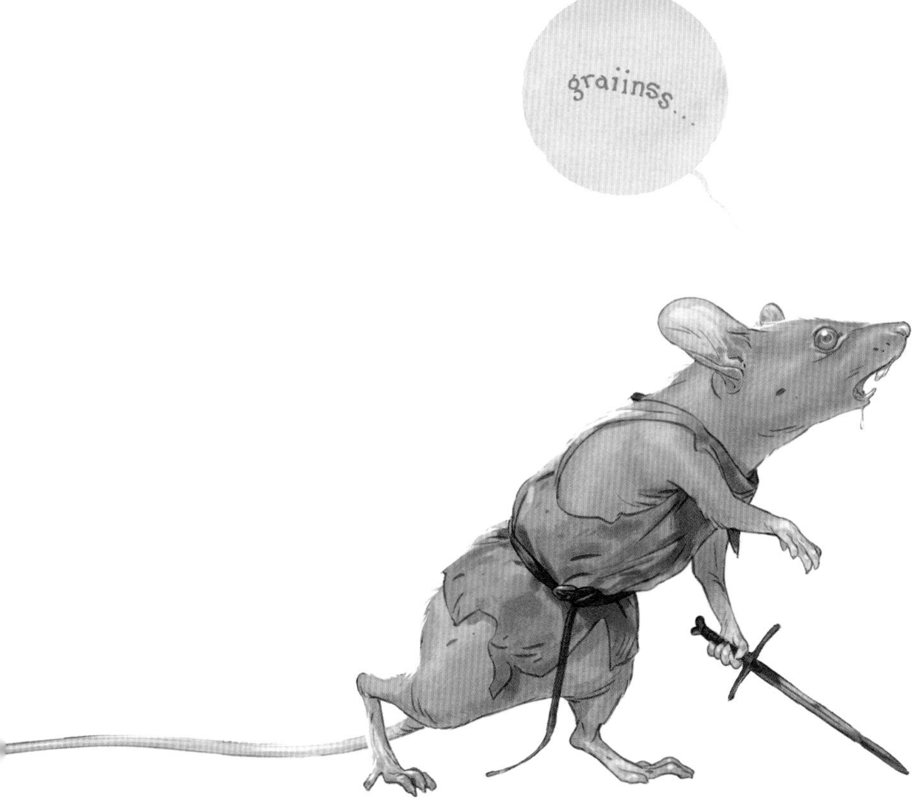
graiinss...

Iguana: "What does that curse do again?"

Rabbit: "According to this tome, it swaps your Wisdom and Charisma stats."

Iguana: "Is he actually trying to chat up that statue?"

Owl: "Hey, handsome, I've not seen *you* around here before."

Iguana: "This is excruciating."

Owl: "*Hoot...* I *love* the strong, silent type..."

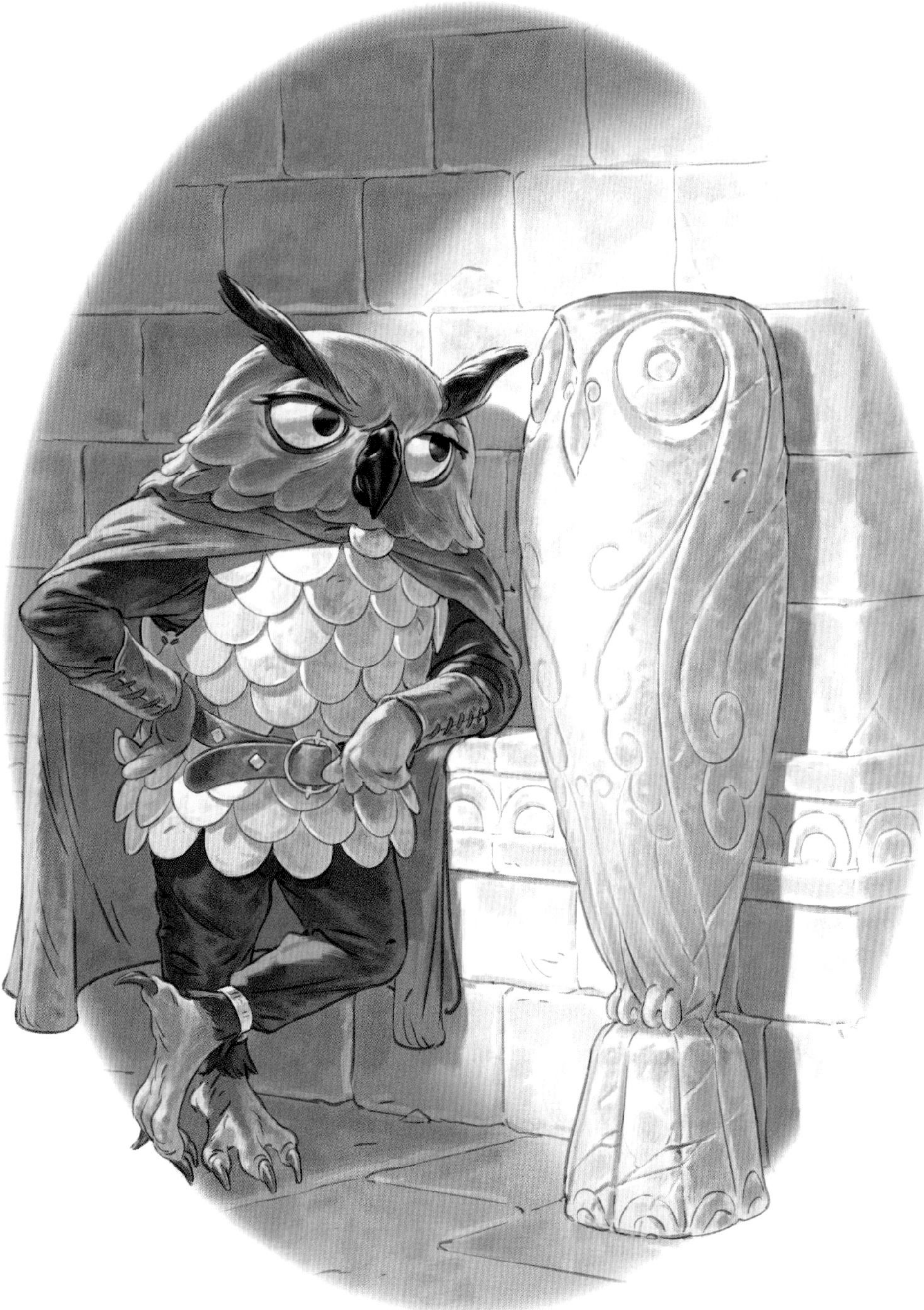

GM: "The giant thunders after you."

Cat: "I hide under the huge armchair."

GM: "Make a Stealth roll."

Cat: "YES! I rolled a 19!"

GM: "A large foot pounds the ground, inches from your hiding spot—"

Cat: "I attack the foot."

GM: *(confused)* "But he hasn't seen y—"

Cat: "I ATTACK THE FOOT!"

GM: *(sighs)* "Roll for your attack..."

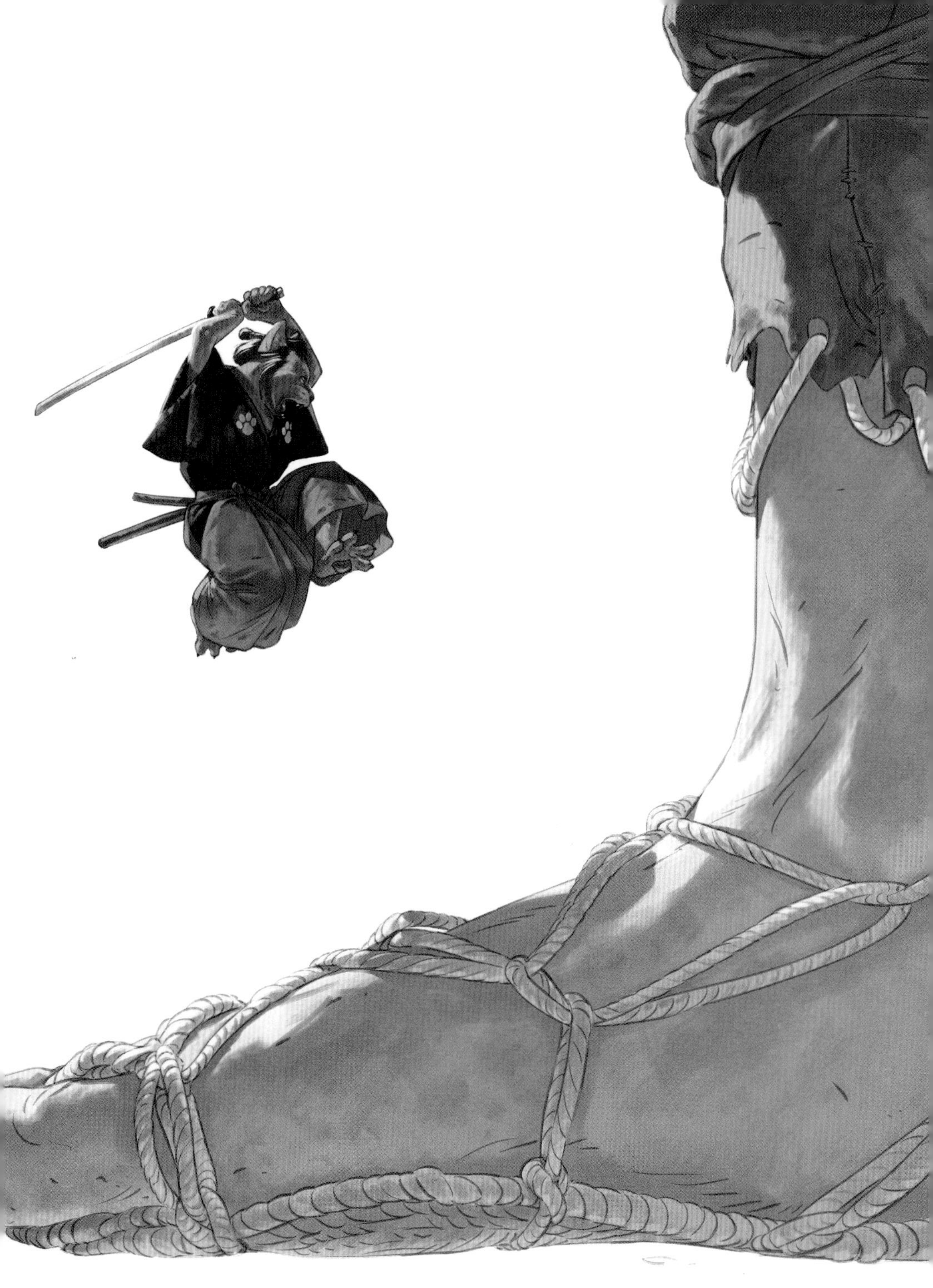

GM: "You find yourselves at the edge of a cliff, faced with a sheer drop onto rocks below."

Dog #1: " I hold the rope for the rest of the party to climb down—"

Dog #2: "Wait! I want to hold the rope!"

Dog #1: "*Back off*, it's mine!"

Dog #2: "No way, it belongs to me!"

GM: "Your argument spirals into an impromptu tug o' war. The pair of you, make a Strength roll..."

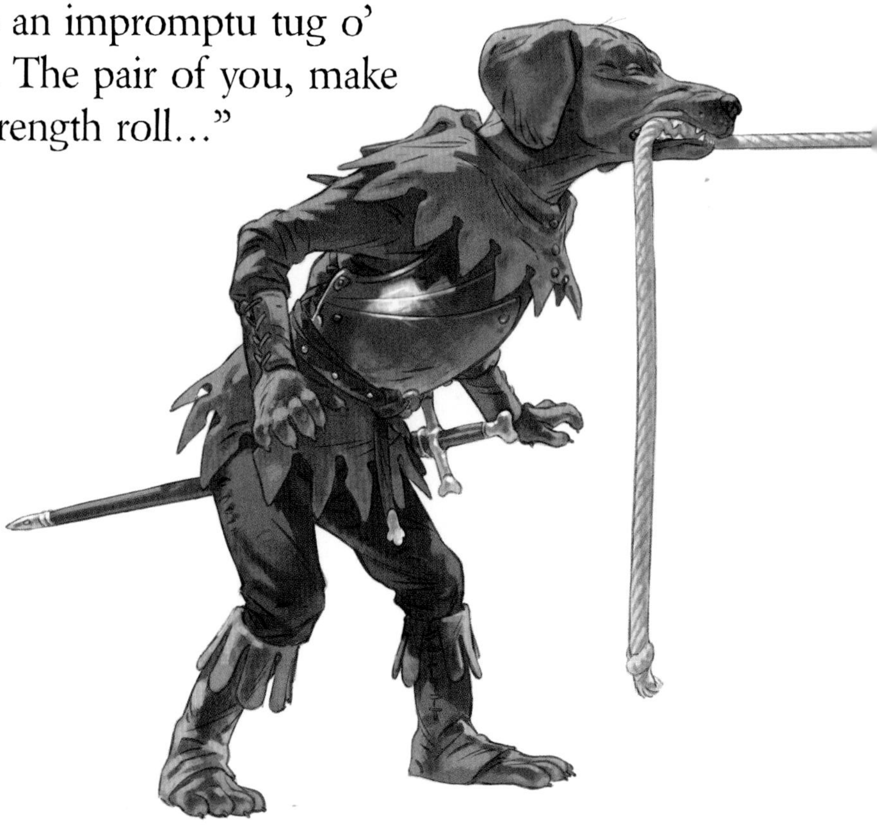

Dog #1: "I got a 14!"

Dog #2: "I *also* got a 14!"

GM: "Roll again…"

Dog #1: "I got an 8!"

Dog #2: "I got an 8 too!"

GM: *(sighs)*

Cat: *(weary)* "I climb down the cliff…"

GM: "The dart flies through the air and—"

Dog: "I run after the dart and bring it back!"

GM: "What? You can't! It's stuck in the bum of the orc it hit."

Dog: "I jump up at the orc, excitedly."

GM: …

GM: "Roll Wisdom."

Dog: "Ah... I got a 4..."

GM: "The orc removes the dart and throws it—"

Dog: "I run after the dart—"

GM: "—into a chasm."

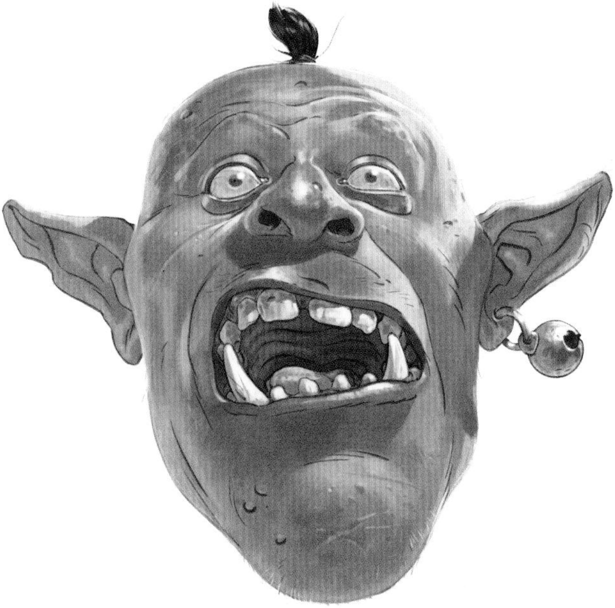
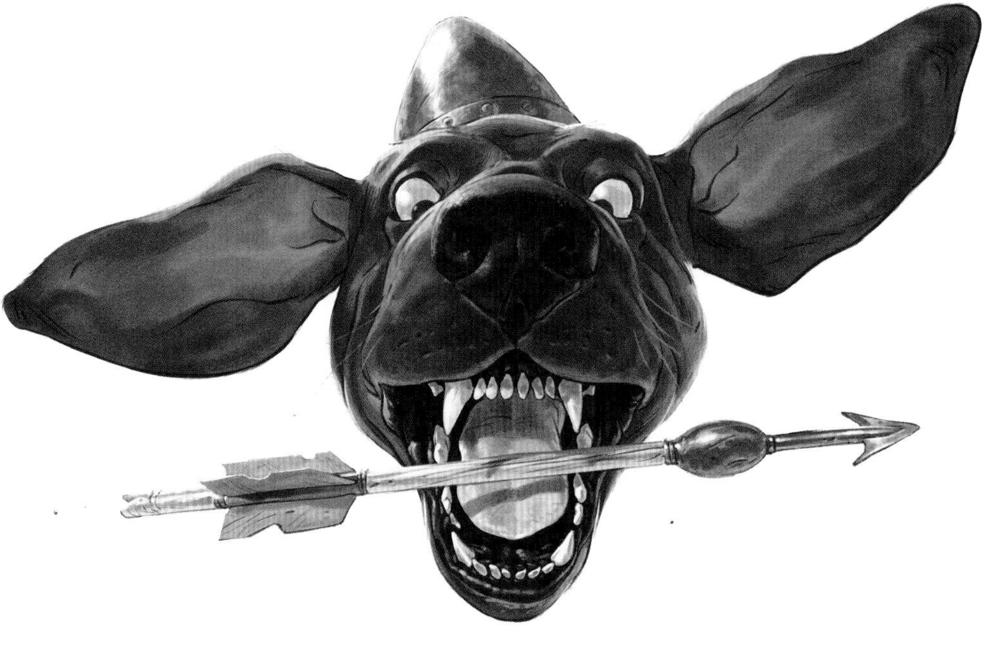

GM: "With a click and a scrape, the door locks behind you and the far wall begins to move swiftly, inexorably closer. You will be crushed to death unless you can find a way to unlock the door from the other side—"

Dog: "I cast *summon animal!*"

GM: "What animal?"

Dog: "A mouse."

GM: "Good choice. The mouse begins to crawl under the door and—"

Cat: "I eat the mouse."

Dog: ...

GM: "A wraith manifests out of the mists in the chamber, and moves towards you."

Dog: "I quickly draw a *protection from evil* circle around me."

GM: "Alright, you draw the circle."

Dog: "Cat, what are you waiting for?"

Cat: *(coughs)* "Erm… well, about that…"

Dog: "Come on, get in the circle, quick!"

Cat: "Many theologians believe this spell's parameters for what is 'evil' are unnecessarily high, having been set in a considerably more puritanical time—"

Dog: *(narrows his eyes)* "You can't cross the line, can you?"

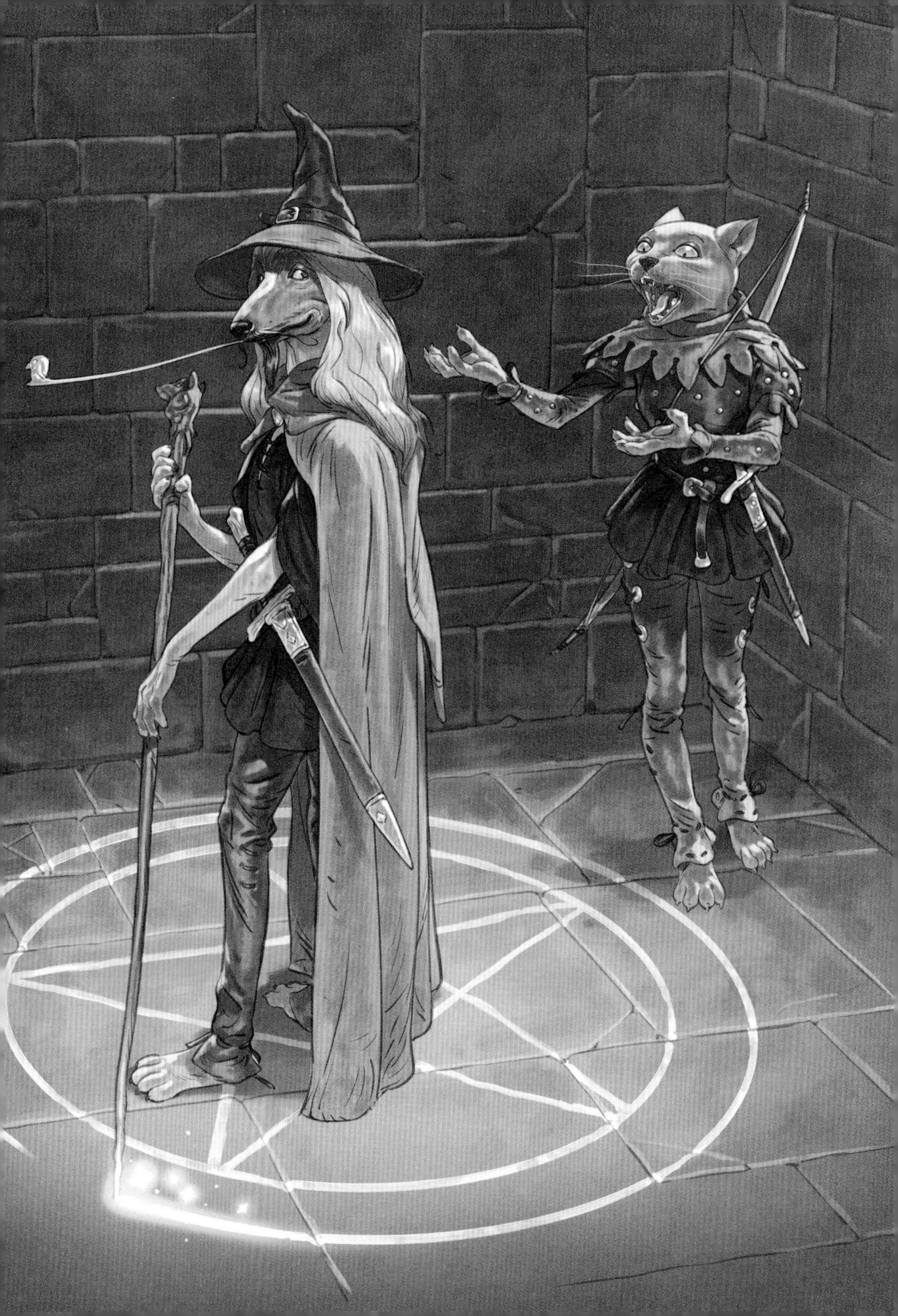

GM: "You spot an owlbear approaching your party."

Cat: "I hide in the shadows."

Dog: "I hide in the shadows too."

GM: "Both of you, make a Stealth roll."

Cat: "A 16! Success!"

Dog: "Erm… I fluffed mine, I got a 3…"

GM: "Cat, even though you are hidden, Dog has unfortunately given you both away."

Cat: "Great… okay I'll cast *fire*—"

Dog: "—BALL!"

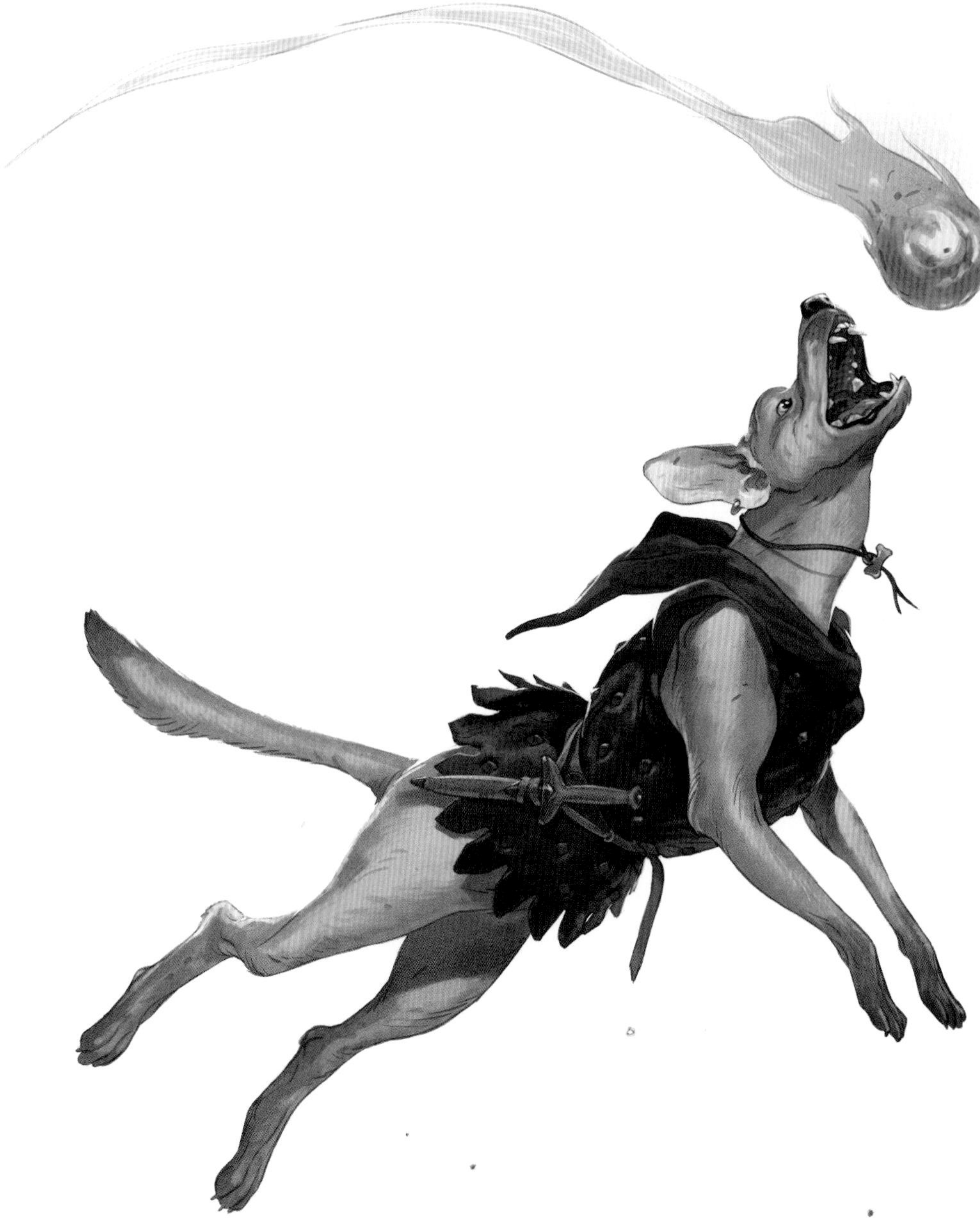

GM: "The road here is well-marked with travellers' footprints, but you cannot immediately discern any from the band of robbers you are pursuing."

Dog: "I sniff the road to see if I can pick up their scents. "

GM: "Roll for Perception."

Dog: "Drat… I got a 2."

GM: "You sniff a footprint, and learn that an elf with diabetes passed by here this morning."

Dog: "I pee on her footprint, and go to sniff others."

GM: "Sure, roll the dice again."

Dog: "Oh, snap, a 6."

GM: "An elderly bard with a fondness for garlic travelled past around midday."

Dog: "I pee on his footprint. Another?"

Cat: *(groans)* "For crying out loud, come on!"

GM: "… and that's 8 points of damage!"

Dog: "Ack! That's me dead then! Goodbye, cruel world!"

GM: "The werewolf slavers over Dog's corpse for a moment before it leaps towards Cat!"

Cat: "Oh, sh—!"

GM: "A hit! Cat, you take 4 points of damage."

Cat: "I run away!"

Dog: …

Dog: *(opens an eye)* "Did it work?"

Werewolf: "Like a charm. You're rid of her."

Dog: "And they all said Play Dead was a pointless skill."

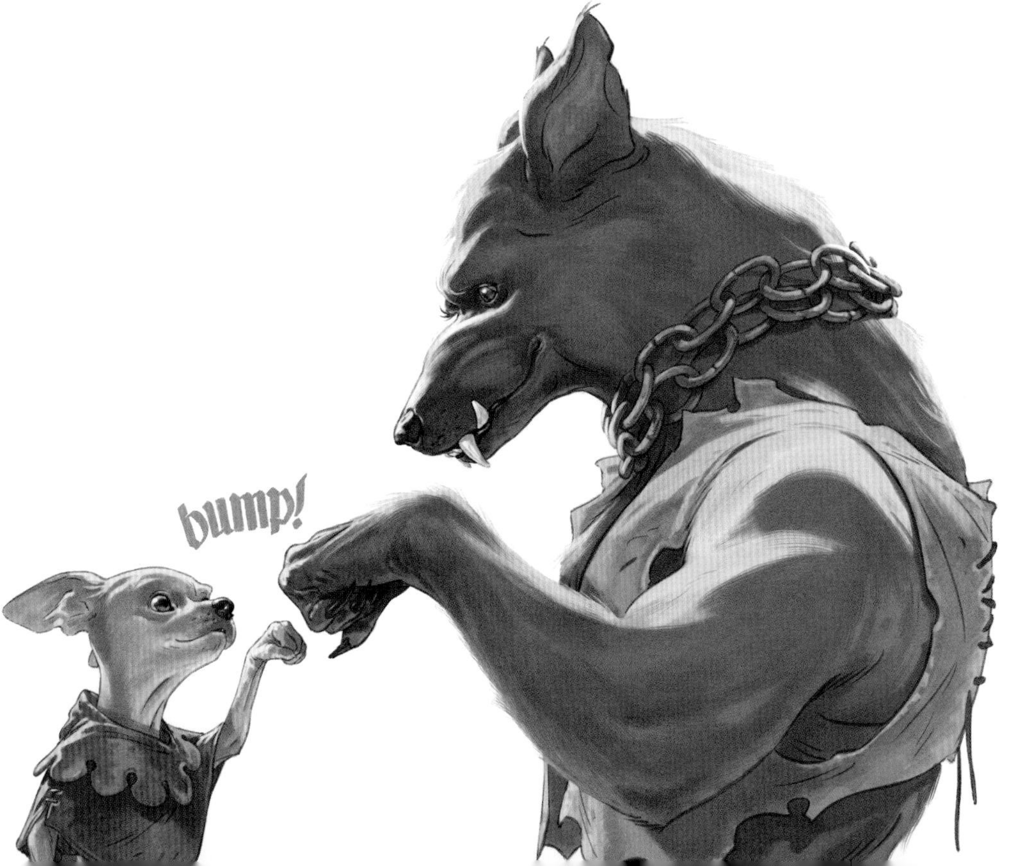
bump!

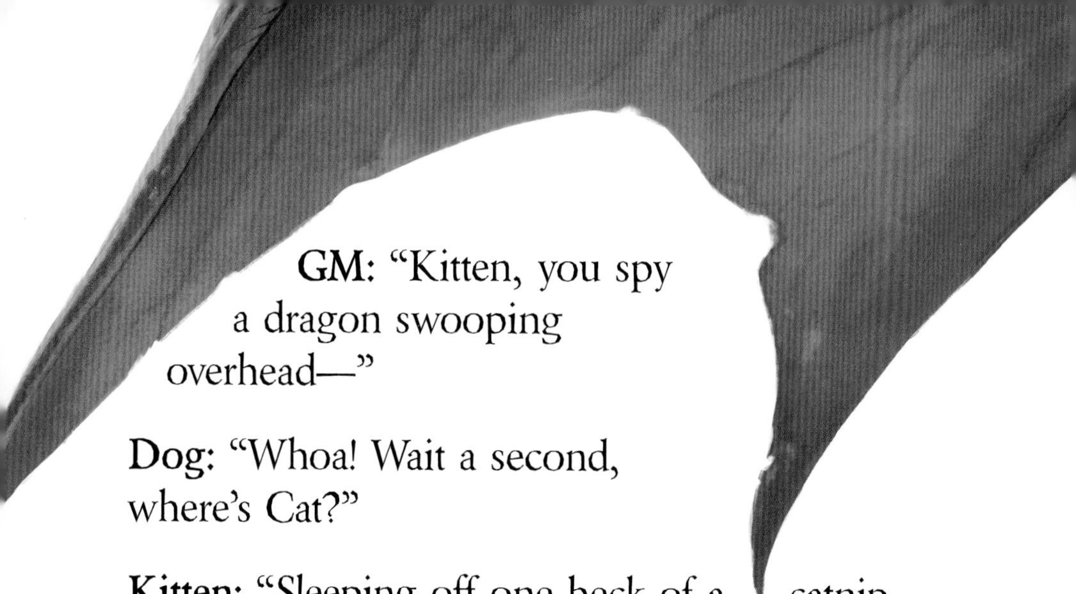

GM: "Kitten, you spy a dragon swooping overhead—"

Dog: "Whoa! Wait a second, where's Cat?"

Kitten: "Sleeping off one heck of a catnip hangover. He said I could sit in for him."

Dog: "No offence, junior, but do you even know how to play?"

Kitten: "I befriend the dragon."

GM: "Roll Charisma."

Dog: "You've got to be joking! That's not how this game works—"

Kitten: "A 19! Too easy..."

GM: "The dragon sits in front of you like an expectant puppy."

Kitten: "I order it to eat Dog."

Dog: "You little bast—"

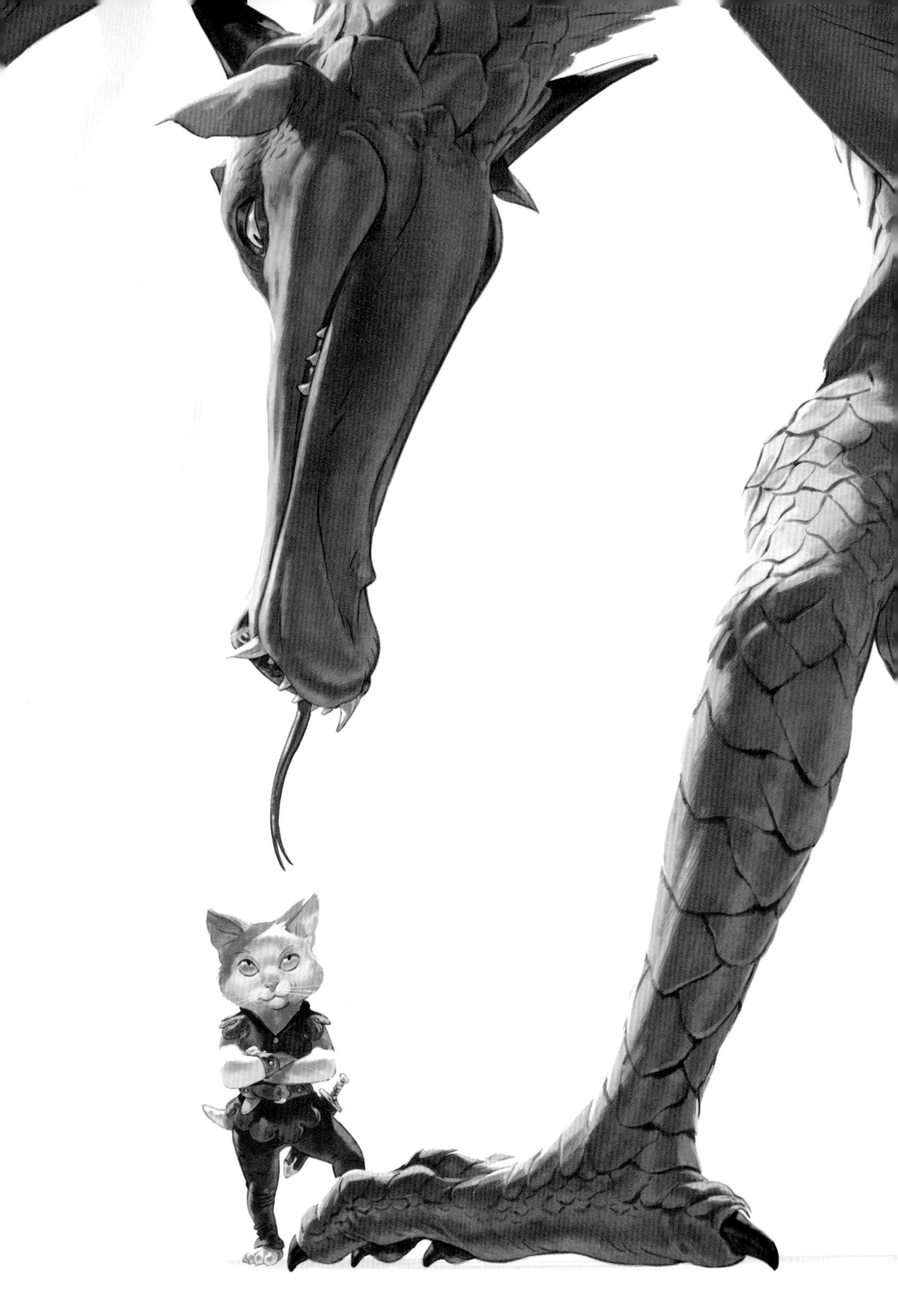

GM: "You see a locked chest."

Dog: "I check for traps."

GM: "Roll the dice."

Dog: "I got a 16. Whatcha got?"

GM: "You notice a trap on the lock."

Dog: "I disarm it."

Cat: "I bat at his paw."

Dog: "What? Hey!"

GM: "Dog, you've now got a -5 modifier to your roll."

Cat: "I crawl between his legs and stick my tail in his face."

Dog: "Cat, stop it! This is delicate work!"

GM: "Make that a -10 modifier."

Dog: "A 12! That's... aw, crap."

GM: "CLICK—"

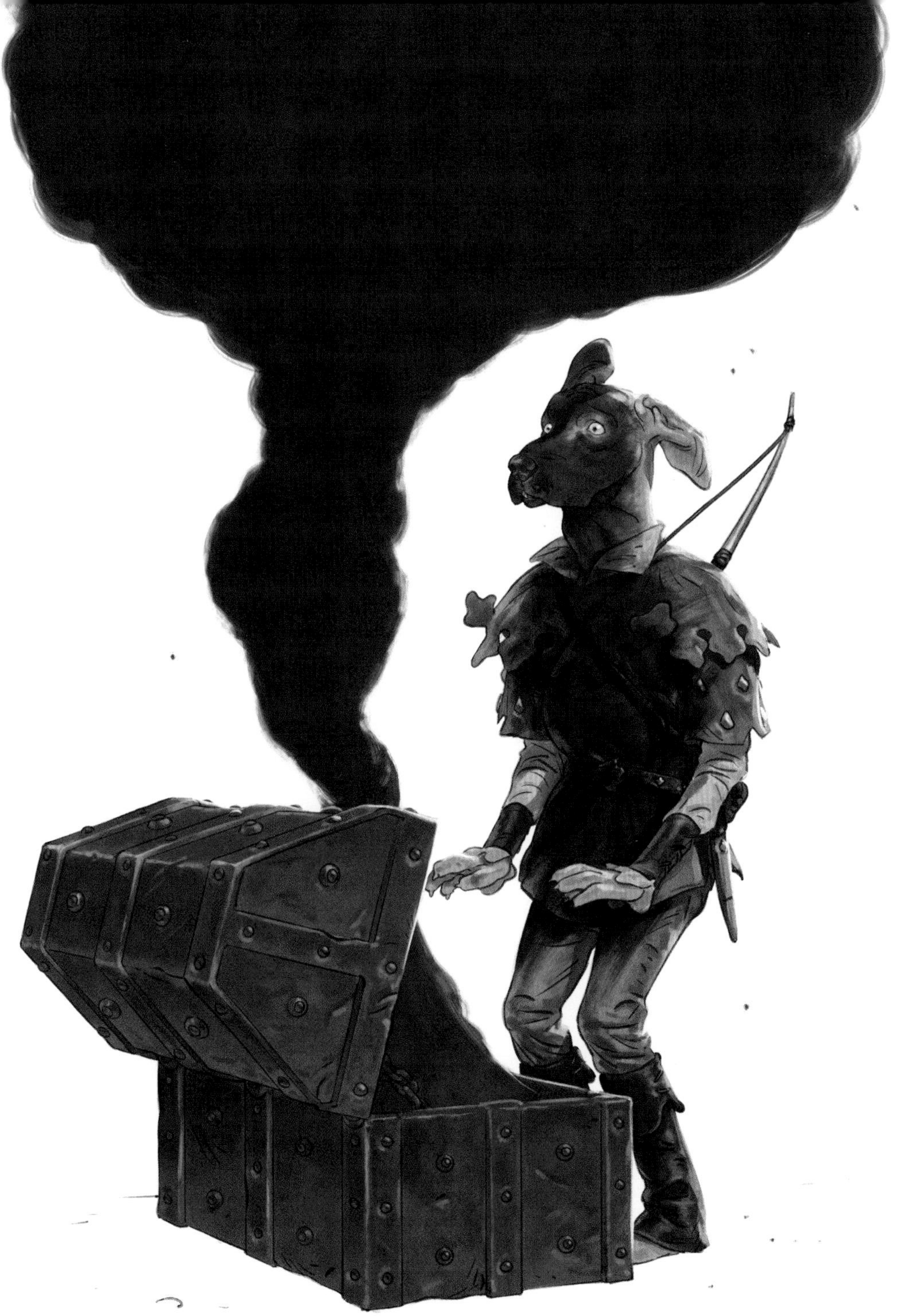

GM: "Entering the dank cave underneath Arawn's castle, you spot a spider—"

Cat: "I leap at the spider!"

GM: "Roll Perception."

Cat: "I got 16. Why? What did I miss?"

GM: "As you sail through the air, you reflect on your rash decision to attack on sight... as the hatchling's gargantuan mother emerges from the shadows behind you."

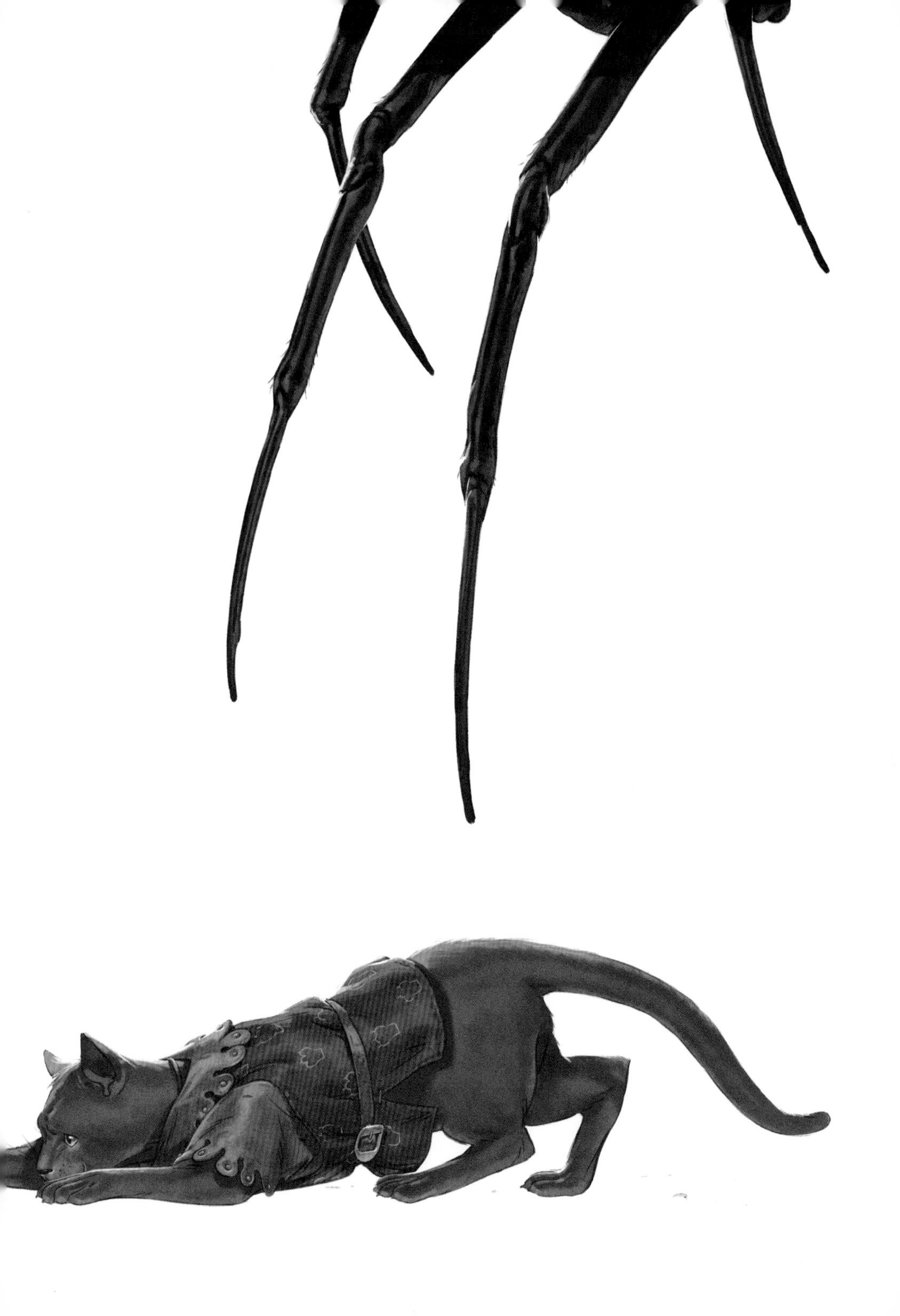

GM: "As you sneak around the back of the fish people's camp, the smell from a pile of rotting food hits you hard."

Dog: "I search the food."

GM: "The odor is stomach-churning, you sure you want to—"

Dog: "I SEARCH THE FOOD."

GM: "Make a Constitution save."

Dog: "No problem, ooh, an 18..."

GM: "Surprisingly, you seem unaffected by the stench as you begin to rummage through it."

Bunny: "What in blazes are you doing?"

Dog: "I roll in the most rotten part of the food."

Bunny: "That's just gross—"

Dog: *(grinning)* "I rub up against Bunny."

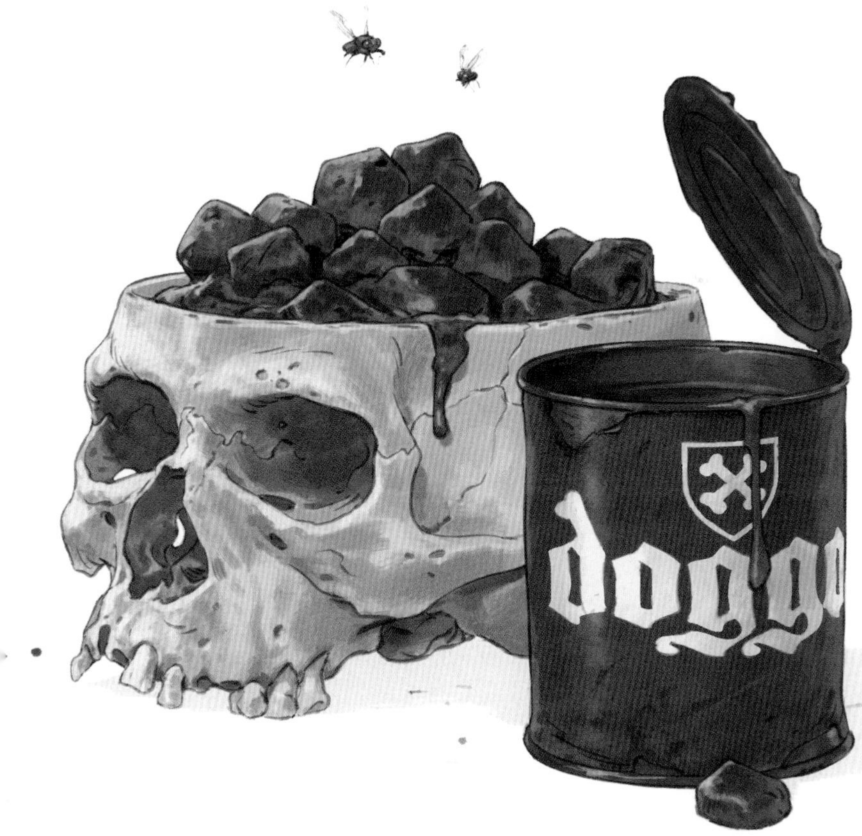
doggo

GM: "You slide the gold coin across the counter towards the merchant. He goes to take it—"

Cat: "I slam my paw down on his hand and stop him."

GM: "Okay, we'll call that an unarmed strike. Roll to hit."

Cat: "19!"

GM: "The merchant stares in shock at you."

Cat: "I smile and slowly let his hand go free."

GM: "Relieved, the merchant goes to take his coin again—"

Cat: "I slam down on his hand once more."

GM: *(sighs)*

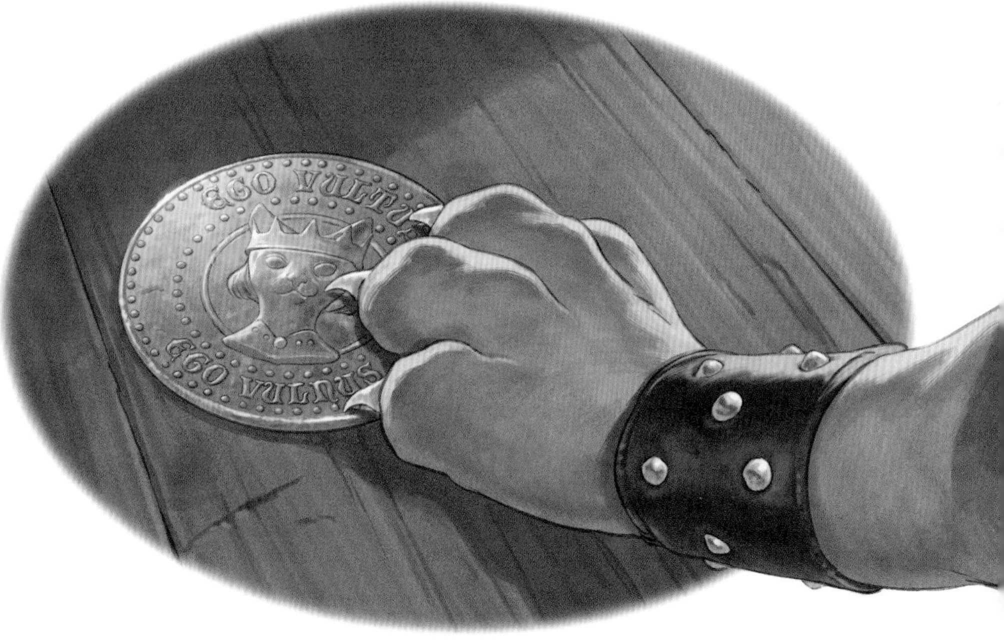

EGO VULTU
EGO VULNUS

GM: "You peek over the fallen rocks at the mouth of the side tunnel and spot the minotaur, dozing upon a hoard of gold coins mixed with the bones of unlucky adventurers."

Rat: *(whispers)* "Here's what we're gonna do. I'll slip in first and cast—"

Cat: "I don't like this plan."

Rat: *(irritated)* "Noted, but this *is* the plan."

Cat: "Well, I don't like it."

Rat: "I cast a *light* spell on the wall next to Cat."

GM: "Cat, roll a Wisdom save."

Cat: "Dash it all, a 1!"

GM: "You're hypnotized by the sudden appearance of a dancing red light on the tunnel wall."

Cat: "Oooh… must catch the light! Must catch it!"

Rat: "Right, where was I?"

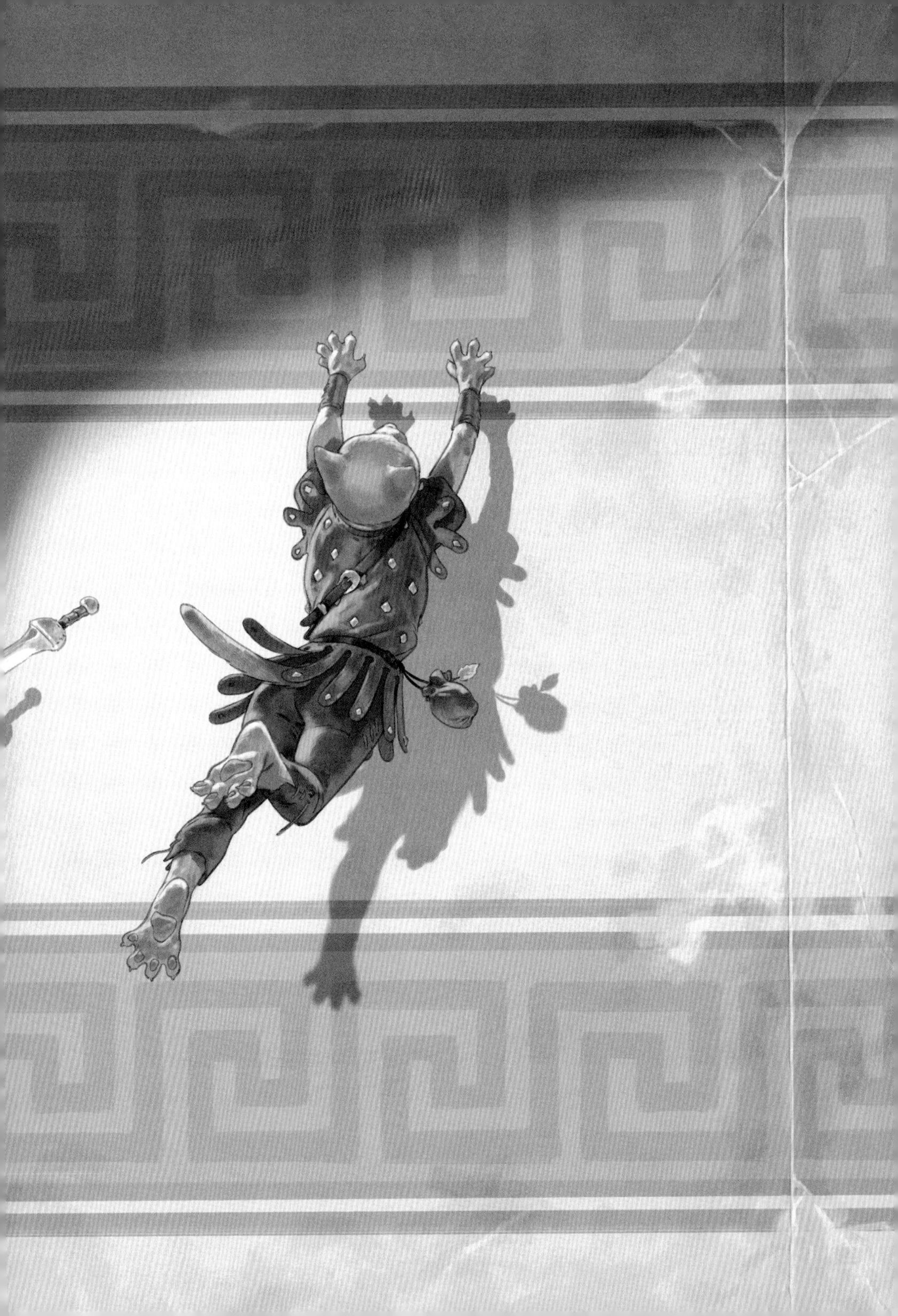

Hedgehog: "I open the second chest."

GM: "A jet of flame takes 5 points off your health."

Troll: "Well, that woz stupid, wasn't it?"

Parakeet: "Is he *still* here?"

Hedgehog: *(sighs)* "Yes."

Troll: "Whatcha gonna do now, losers?"

Hedgehog: "That's it! I cast *magic boulder.*"

Parakeet: "What are you doing?"

Hedgehog: "The only thing *worth* doing with trolls."

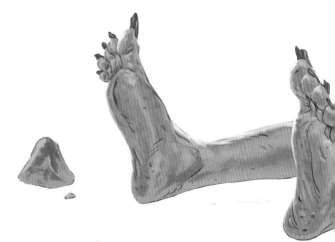

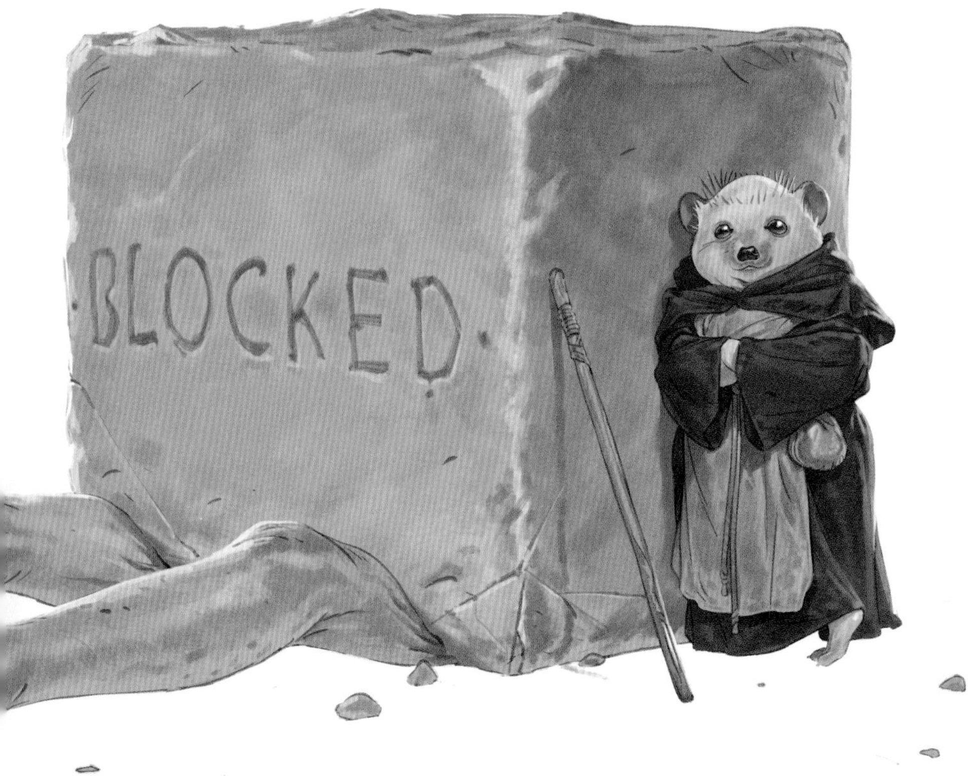
BLOCKED

GM: "With the last swing of your sword, the skeletal knight smashes into pieces that scatter across the stone floor."

Dog: "Search the remains."

GM: "Roll Perception."

Dog: "I got a 2—"

GM: "You find only old bones."

Dog: "We've hit the jackpot, lads! Bag this and let's head on home."

GM: "What about the rest of the quest?"

Dog: "Forget it. I've got what I came for."

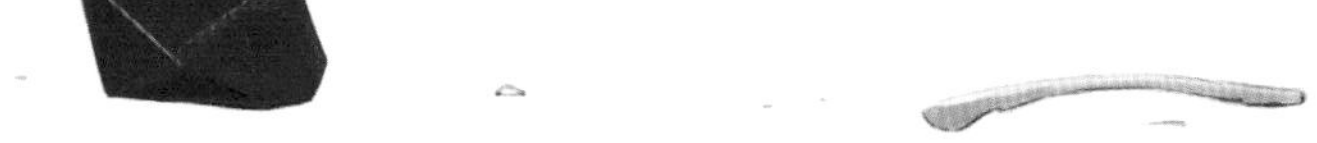

GM: "The last frost giant falls! The Ice Orb sits upon the altar, unguarded at last. Once you destroy it, your quest will be complete, for you will have banished the endless winter that plagues your once-verdant land."

Dog: "It's so shiny..."

Cat: "Wait! The prophecy said it was dangerous! If you touch it directly, you'll—"

Dog: "I lick the Orb."

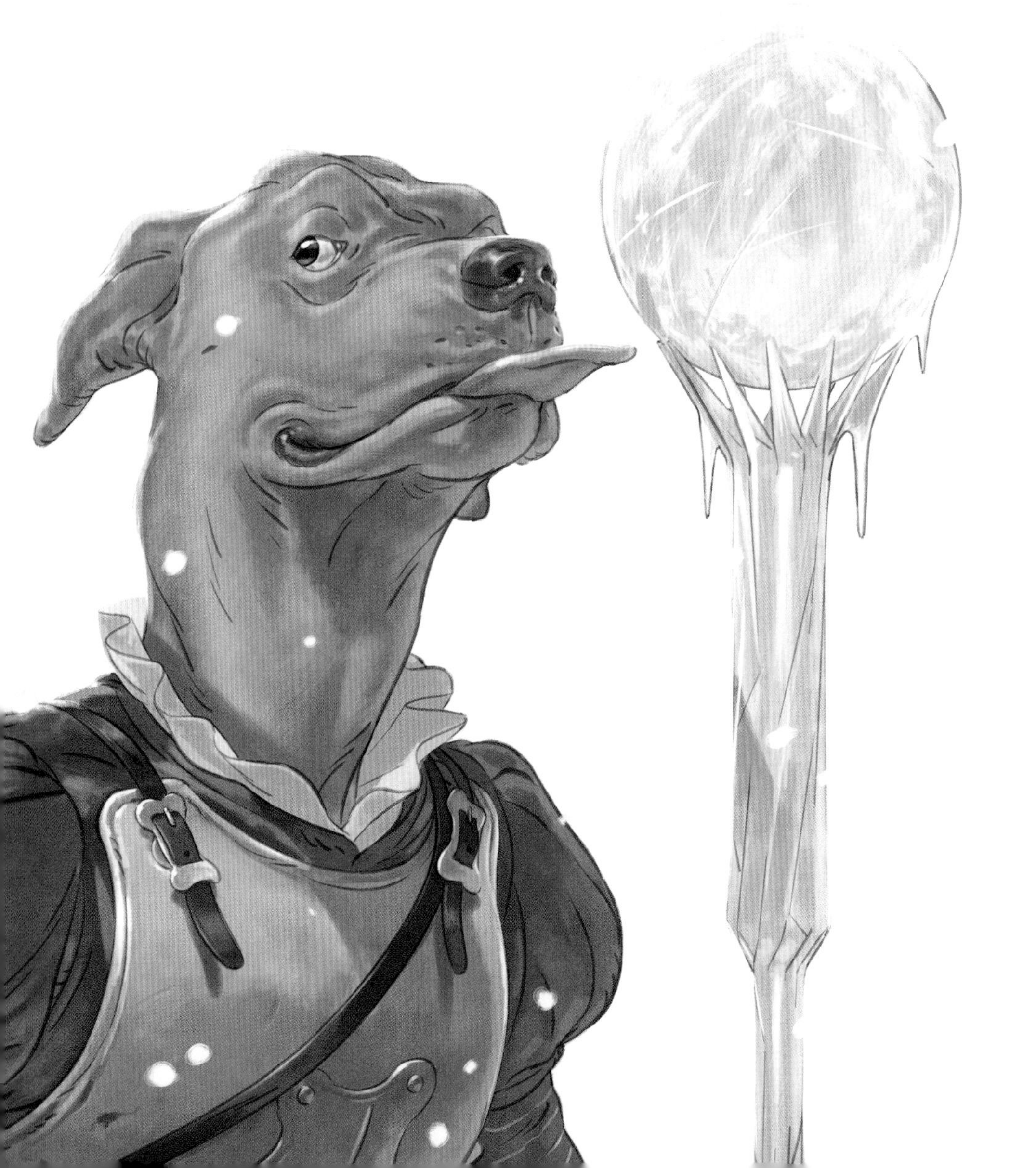

About the Creators

Andi Ewington (@AndiEwington) has written numerous comic titles including *Forty-Five45*, *S6X*, *Sunflower*, *Red Dog*, *Dark Souls II*, *Just Cause 3*, *Freeway Fighter*, and *Vikings*. Andi lives in Surrey, England with his wife, two children and a plethora of childhood RPGs and *Choose Your Own Adventure* gamebooks he refuses to part with.

Rhianna Pratchett (@RhiPratchett) has worked on titles such as *Heavenly Sword*, *Mirror's Edge*, *Overlord*, and the *Tomb Raider* reboot. In the world of comics, Rhianna has created stories for DC, Dark Horse, Dynamite and Kodansha, during which her favourite achievement was having Lara Croft fight bad guys on the London Underground whilst dressed as one of the Bennet sisters.

In film and TV, Rhianna has worked with Motive Pictures, Film4, New Regency, Complete Fiction and The Bureau on multiple adaptations and original commissions.

Most recently, Rhianna wrote the Fighting Fantasy novel *Crystal of Storms* for Scholastic.

Calum Alexander Watt (@CalumAWatt) is a freelance concept artist and illustrator working in the entertainment industry. He has created costume concepts for Neill Blomkamp (*Alien* and *Zygote*), Lucasfilm (*Star Wars: The Rise of Skywalker, Solo: A Star Wars Story*), character designs for Pixar (*Lightyear*) and storyboarded for Blur Studios and Tim Miller (*Terminator* and *Love, Death and Robots*). He lives and works in the UK, somewhere near the sea with his wife, twin daughters and 2.9 cats.

Alex de Campi (@alexdecampi) is a thriller writer with an extensive backlist of critically-acclaimed graphic novels including Eisner-nominated heist noir *Bad Girls* (Simon & Schuster). Her most recent books were pulp horror graphic novel *Dracula, Motherf**ker* (Image Comics), sci-fi thriller *Madi: Once Upon A Time in the Future* co-written with Duncan Jones (Z2 Comics), and *True War Stories*, an anthology of soldiers' deployment tales.

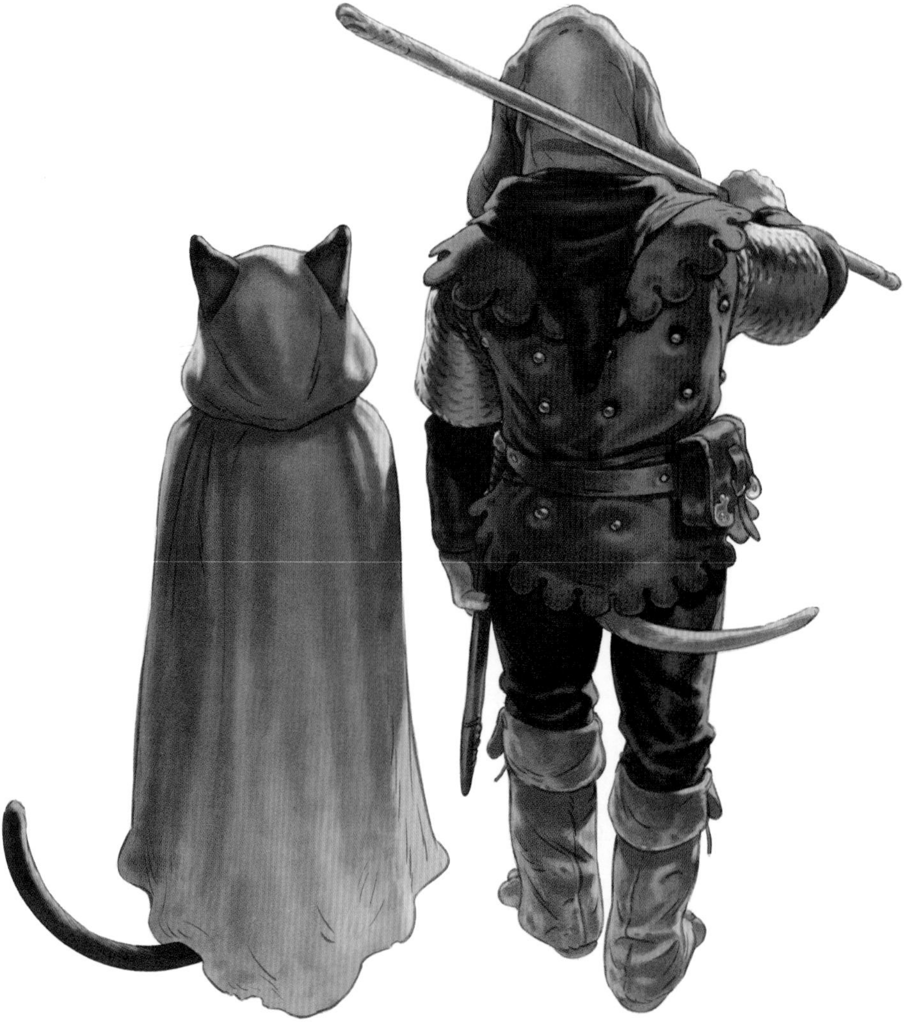

Creative Director and CEO: Jason Kingsley
Chief Technical Officer: Chris Kingsley
Head of Publishing: Ben Smith
Publishing Manager: Beth Lewis
Editorial: David Thomas Moore, Michael Rowley, Jim Killen & Amy Borsuk
Publishing Coordinator: Owen Johnson
Production Manager: Dagna Dlubak
Graphic Design: Sam Gretton, Oz Osborne & Gemma Sheldrake
PR and Marketing: Hanna Waigh and Rosie Peat
Archivist: Charlene Taylor

ISBN: 978-1-78108-922-4

Published by Rebellion, Riverside House,
Osney Mead, Oxford, UK. OX2 OES
www.rebellion.co.uk

Printed in Turkey by Imago
1st Printing: September 2021
10 9 8 7 6 5 4 3 2 1

To find out more, visit RebellionPublishing.com

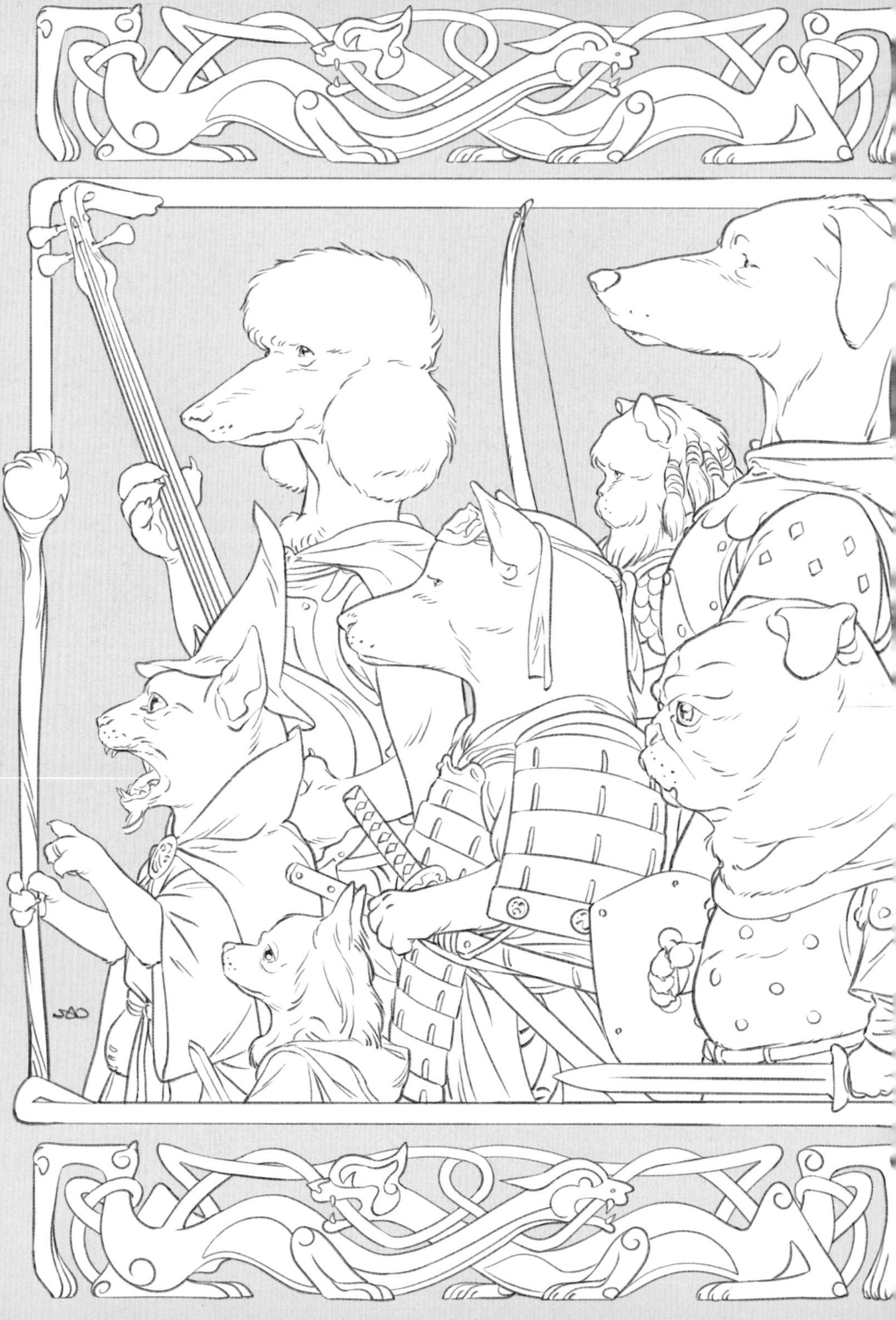